Alien Abduction

By Sean Keyhoe

***

Alien Abduction

By Sean Keyhoe

***

© 2013 Sean Keyhoe – All Rights Reserved Worldwide

Table of Contents

Introduction

   Chapter 1 - Where it Really Started p. 7

   Chapter 2 - Financial Considerations p. 68

   Chapter 3 - Dreaming of Aliens p. 92

   Chapter 4 - Alien Abduction Case 3 p. 98

   Chapter 5 - Alien Abduction Case 4 p. 103

   Chapter 6 - Alien Abduction Case 5 p. 110

   Chapter 7 - More Problems with Memories p. 124

   Chapter 8 - Messages Delivered p. 136

   Chapter 9 - Alien Artifacts p. 140

   Chapter 10 - A Worldwide Phenomenon p. 146

   Afterword

Appendix 1

Appendix 2

Appendix 3

Bibliography & References

Introduction

If I had to choose two words to describe the topic of Alien Abduction, I would use the words controversial and demanding.

Alien abduction is certainly controversial; you have a range of opinion that runs from those who dismiss outright anything to do with aliens. They reject the topic on principle and will not listen to anything related to the subject. This may be out of fear, frustration or both. Whatever their reasons, these individuals are simply not interested.

On the other end of the spectrum you have people who have highly detailed theories and explanations for what alien abductions are all about. They will argue about how prevalent abductions are and what are the specific reasons behind them.

I would also describe the topic as demanding for several reasons. The sheer volume of information that is available on this topic is staggering. It is next to impossible to examine the subject without partially delving into the overall topic of Aliens and UFOs in a much broader sense.

Taking those challenges into consideration I have attempted to present this subject in a way that is interesting, objective and useful for anyone who may have an interest in this area. Even though some of the specific accounts are well known I have attempted to provide new insights and data that has never been published before. Others accounts are very new or quite obscure; providing new insights for readers of all backgrounds.

So it is my hope that this book will provide valuable content to anyone and everyone; from those with a mere passing interest to those who want to delve into the subject with a fine-tooth comb. I hope you will find this information, as I did, interesting, intriguing and enlightening.

~ Sean Keyhoe

Chapter 1 - Where it Really Started

There is evidence of alien encounters and possible alien abductions dating back hundreds of years but if you really wanted to pinpoint the starting point of 'modern-day' alien abductions, you would have to start with the case of Betty and Barney Hill. This case is well known to almost anyone with even a passing interest in UFOs or Aliens. A made for TV movie was produced starring James Earl Jones as Barney Hill and the State of New Hampshire even erected a type of monument for passers-by at the incident location as in the following image:

It occurred in a place called Indian Head, New Hampshire; it is often considered the sight of the first recorded instance of alien contact with humans. Betty and Barney Hill were driving home one night from a visit to Canada, returning to the United States on the night of, and early morning of, September 19th to 20th, 1961 at which time they were startled by a brilliant light.

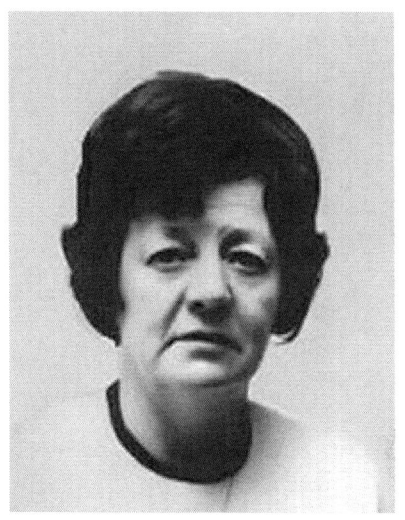

Betty Hill

Betty Hill: "As it came out over the highway, we stopped, we looked up and we could see a curved picture window with a red light on each side. So Barney took the binoculars, he got out of the car and tried to identify this craft. And he could see a group of men standing in the window looking down at him; and at that moment he became fearful, he had the impression they were trying to capture him."

Scared, he jumped back into their car and they raced away from the scene. But when they arrived home, they discovered strange marks on the hood of their car and a mysterious substance on Betty's dress. They also could not account for three hours that had passed.

Betty Hill: "Somehow we just had a feeling of contamination, so I said to Barney, 'This sounds weird.' And I don't know why I'm saying that. We'd been touched, somehow we'd been touched."

The Hill's experience led them to seek the help of noted psychiatrist, Dr. Benjamin Simon. Their hypnotherapy sessions revealed a trauma unlike any recorded before. In fact they were so traumatic that Betty and Barney were prevented from hearing their own tapes of the sessions until months later. The news of their experience quickly leaked out triggering a frenzy of media interest.

Betty Hill: "Well, we became known almost immediately. Barney and I would go out to eat and people would come up and ask for our autograph."

Betty kept the dress from her experience and showed it to investigators and reporters. Portions of the dress had been stained pink. She even cut out a portion of the dress that was stained and sent it to a lab to be analyzed.

Betty Hill: "You can see here the blue and this is where it became stained by the pink powdered substance. This is the place where I cut out and sent it to a lab. They were unable to analyze it; they have no idea what caused the pink stain."

The Actual Transcripts of Barney Hill

When Betty and Barney Hill underwent hypnosis, recordings were made of the sessions. A number of the session recordings of Barney Hill found their way into public records and here for the first time on Kindle are transcripts[1] of some of those sessions.[2] The hypnotist is

---

[1] For more transcripts of both Betty and Barney's hypnosis sessions, you can find additional details from the book: 'Interrupted Journey' by John G. Fuller.

[2] A larger amount of these sessions were originally transcribed and published in the book 'Interrupted Journey' by John G. Fuller but these are my own transcriptions from listening to recordings first hand.

Dr. Benjamin Simon and the sessions were conducted from January 4th, 1964 to June 6th, 1964.

Barney Hill

Transcript of some of Barney Hill's Hypnosis Sessions:

Hypnotist: Go deeper and deeper, deeper asleep. All asleep. Deeper and deeper. Fully relaxed, all nothing but relaxed, relaxed. You're comfortable, relaxed. You will not be anxious or distressed but you will remember everything and you will tell me everything.

Barney Hill: Yes. I think I will stop, I will stop and I have not stopped, and Betty said, 'look there's a star moving'. And I looked and I see a star. Funny, but I said, 'Betty, that's a satellite.' We are seeing a satellite. And then I pulled over to the side of the road and Betty jumped out her side, on her side with the binoculars and I got the chain and I hooked it to the dog on her collar and I said, 'come on Delsy, let's get out'. And she jumps out and I look towards the sky and I looked back to Delsey and walk her around the trunk of the car and I was saying, 'hurry up Betty so I can get a look.'

And Betty passes the binoculars to me and I see that not a set of lights. It's, it's an airplane. It's an airplane you can see. I think you can see the rows of windows and it is an airplane and I tell Betty this and give the binoculars back to her and I am satisfied. And I drive and Betty is still looking, she says, 'Barney that is not a plane, it's still following us.' And I stop and I look and I see the star up there off in the distance; so I search for a place to pull off the road. And I see a dirt road to the right of this main highway and I think this is a good place I can pull off. And if any car comes, it won't strike me.

And I am deeply, this is strange because it's still there and Betty said, I think she said, I'm mad with her I said. I believe Betty is trying to make me think this is a flying saucer.

Hypnotist: Was it light enough to see?

Barney Hill: I was just a light moving through the sky and I heard no noise and I think, 'this is ridiculous. And Betty this is not a flying saucer, what are you doing this for? You want to believe in this thing and I don't'. And I can't hear any sound.

Hypnotist: No sound whatever?

Barney Hill: I can't. I want to hear a jet, oh I want to hear a jet so badly, I want to hear it.

Hypnotist: Why do you want to hear a jet?

Barney Hill: Because Betty is making me mad; she is making me angry. She's saying, 'look at that, it's strange it's not a plane, look at it' and I keep thinking it's got to be - I want to hear a hum. I want to hear a motor.

Hypnotist: How far away was it?

Barney Hill: It was, oh, it wasn't far. It was about a thousand feet I guess.

Hypnotist: A thousand feet.

Barney Hill: A thousand feet.

Hypnotist: Did it go back and forth or did it go in circles like a...

It would go towards the west and without looking as if to turn it would come straight back..if it..I think of a paddle and a ball with a rubber...you hit the ball and the ball goes straight out and comes straight back without a circle and I think only a jet could fly that fast. And I am hoping I can find a good place where I can really see this thing, whatever it is. And I see a wigwam and I recognize this place, and I though first I said...let's ,...in the barren house.

Hypnotist: What is this place?

Barney Hill: It is an area.

Hypnotist: What is this place?

Barney Hill: It is Indian Head, I had been there before and I feel comforted but I see a familiar face, and I think I will get a good look at this because Betty was very annoying, she was annoyed. By telling me look and I can't look up I have to drive the car and I want to wake up.

Hypnotist: You're not going to wake up, you're in a deep sleep you're comfortable. Relax, this is not going to trouble you. Go on. You can remember everything now.

Barney Hill: It's better than my right. Gosh; what is it, and I try to maintain control so Betty cannot tell I'm scared. God, I'm scared.

Hypnotist: It's alright, you can go along, you can experience it, it will not hurt you any.

Barney Hill: I gotta get my gun; oooh, gotta get my gun, OOOHHH!

Hypnotist: Alright, alright.

Barney Hill: I GOTTA GET MY GUN!

Hypnotist: Go to sleep, deeper breaths now.

(Barney starts crying and gasping)

Hypnotist: Calm now, relaxed. Deeply relaxed.

(Barney starts to calm down.)

Hypnotist: Deeply relaxed, you'll not have to make any outcry. But you can remember it now, keep remembering. You feel you have to get your gun; this is going to harm you, you felt.

Barney Hill: I opened the trunk of my car, I get it, I get back in the car.

Hypnotist: Alright just keep reasonably calm.

Barney Hill: I put it in my coat and then I get out with the binoculars and it's there and I look, and I look, and it's just over, and I think I'm not afraid, I will shoot it down, I am not afraid and I look, I look out and I walk across the road. There it is up there; OH GOD DAMMIT...

Hypnotist: Calm down, calm down, it's there, you did see it but it's not gonna hurt you, go on.

Barney Hill: Why is it...go away...look at it...and there's a man there.

Hypnotist: Calm, calm, it's not gonna hurt you.

Barney Hill: And there's a man...and he's, he, is he a captain? - what is he...it is gonna look at me.

Hypnotist: Just a minute let's go back a little bit now. You say it's there, did you say it was a thousand feet away, a thousand yards?

Barney Hill: Oh no, it doesn't look that far, it's very big and it's not that far. And I can see it tilted towards me.

Hypnotist: It tilted, what does it look like now, when you say tilted, did you see windows?

Barney Hill: It looks like a big, big, pancake with windows and rows of windows and lights of- not , not lights just one huge light.

Hypnotist: Rows of windows like a commercial plane?

Barney Hill: Rows of windows, they're not like a commercial plane because they curve around to the sides of this pancake and I say, 'my God no, I have to stay right here, this can't be true, this isn't fair'. It's still there, and I look up and down the road, can't somebody come and tell me this is not there; it can't be. And it's all…

Hypnotist: You're still asleep but you can see it all clearly.

Barney Hill: It's there.

Hypnotist: You're sure it's there?

Barney Hill: Yeah.

Hypnotist: You weren't having a dream?

Barney Hill: It's there.

Hypnotist: You had no sleep that evening?

Barney Hill: I touched my right arm, it's not my right it's my left arm and then I touch my right arm, and that's my left arm, I come through.

Hypnotist: You're clear now, you're relaxed.

Barney Hill: It's still there. If I let my binoculars fall and dangle from my neck and then start over again, maybe it won't be there, but it is. Why? What do they want? What do they want? They,…one… person looks for me, he's friendly looking and he's looking at me over his right shoulder and he's smiling but, but that…

Hypnotist: Could you see him clearly?

Barney Hill: Yes, I thought

Hypnotist: What's his face like, what's it make you think of?

Barney Hill: It's round, I think of, I think of a red head Irishman, I don't know why. But I think I know why. Because Irish are usually hostile to Negroes and when I see a friendly Irish person I react to it by thinking I will be friendly. And I think this one that is looking over his shoulder is friendly.

Hypnotist: You say looking over his shoulder, was he facing away from you?

Barney Hill: Yes, he was facing a wall.

Hypnotist: You saw him through this window? You said there was a row of windows.

Barney Hill: It was a row of windows, just a huge row of windows; only divided by…uh…struts or structures that prevented it from being one solid window or then it would have been one solid window and this evil face on the…he looks like a German Nazi…he is a Nazi.

Hypnotist: He is a Nazi? Did he have on a uniform?

Barney Hill: Yes

Hypnotist: What kind of uniform.

Barney Hill: It was black, he had a black scarf around his neck dangling over his left shoulder.

Hypnotist: You pointed it out as if it was on you.

Barney Hill: I never noticed that before.

Hypnotist: A dark scarf on the neck. How could you see these figures so clearly at this distance?

Barney Hill: I was looking at them with binoculars.

Hypnotist: Oh. Did they have faces like other people? You say one reminded you of a red-headed Irishman.

Barney Hill: His eyes were slanted, I see it oh, his eyes are slanted but not like a Chinese.

Hypnotist: What was Betty doing all this time?

Barney Hill: I'm not close to her, I don't know.

Hypnotist: You're out there by yourself now? You don't think of her, isn't she saying anything?

Barney Hill: I can't hear her.

Hypnotist: Did you make any outcry to her? The way you did to me?

Barney Hill: I,I,..I can't remember, I don't know, I did not.

Hypnotist: You would remember it if you did.

Barney Hill: I did not. I know this, this creature, this leader is telling me something.

Hypnotist: He's telling you something. How? How is he getting it to you?

Barney Hill: I can see it in his face.

Hypnotist: You see his lips move? Yes?

Barney Hill: No his lips aren't moving.

Hypnotist: Yes go on. He'll tell you.

Barney Hill: He's looking at me.

Hypnotist: What did he tell you?

Barney Hill: Stay there and keep looking, just keep looking and stay there and just keep looking, just keep looking.

Hypnotist: Could you hear him tell you?

Barney Hill: …ah I gotta pull these binoculars away from my eyes cuz if I don't I'll just keep staying there.

Hypnotist: Could you hear him tell you this?

Barney Hill: Ah no, he didn't say it.

Hypnotist: You felt he said it.

Barney Hill: I know.

Hypnotist: You know he did.

Barney Hill: It's there, yeah, just stay there he's saying to me.

Hypnotist: Alright.

Barney Hill: How'd he get my head. Don't pull the binoculars away. God give me strength. Pull them down. RUN! PULL THE BINOCULARS DOWN AND RUN. God, If there's a God give me strength, I've gotta get away (hysterical)ohh, oh..you gotta get away from me..

Hypnotist: Alright, calm down, calm down.

Barney Hill: I'm dying,..I'm gonna get away.

Hypnotist: How could you be sure he's telling you this? Calm down you're still in sleep. How could you be sure he was telling you this?

Barney Hill: His eyes, his eyes. I never seen those eyes before.

Hypnotist: But you said they were friendly, you said they were friendly.

Barney Hill: Oh the, not the leaders, they weren't looking over his shoulders.

Hypnotist: Oh I see, the leader was the; how did you know the other one was the leader?

Barney Hill: Because everybody moved; everyone was standing there looking at me, but everybody moved to these leaders or in the back or they went to this big board; it looked like a board and only this one with the black, black shiny jacket and the scarf stayed at the window. I'm driving.

Hypnotist: You're going back into the car now?

Barney Hill: Yes.

Hypnotist: You put down your binoculars did you?

Barney Hill: I got em down, yes.

Hypnotist: Then you got into the car, you didn't speak to Betty.

Barney Hill: I'm getting a hold of myself. I'm saying hold to myself; don't panic, you've got great fortitude, you can drive the car and if I... I told Betty to look out and the object was still around us. I could feel it around us. I saw it when we passed by, the object, when I got into the car, it had swung around so that it was out there. I knew it was out there. It's out there.. but I'm not aware...funny.

Hypnotist: Yes, speak a little louder.

Barney Hill: I know, those three. Oh, those eyes, they're there in my brain. Oh please can I wake up?

Hypnotist: Stay asleep a little longer, we'll get through this now alright. We'll get through it alright. All of your feelings forming; they won't upset you so much.

Barney Hill: Isn't that funny; oh the woods.

Hypnotist: Yes

Barney Hill: That crazy dog. She stays in the car all the time. Isn't that funny. She stays in the car.

Hypnotist: She doesn't bark; do anything?

Barney Hill: She just stays there.

Hypnotist: What about Betty?

Barney Hill: I don't know.

Hypnotist: Isn't she saying anything?

Barney Hill: No. I don't understand, are we being robbed? I...I don't know.

Hypnotist: What makes you think you're being robbed?

Barney Hill: I know what's in my mind and I don't want to say it.

Hypnotist: Well you can say t to me, you can say it now.

Barney Hill: They're men; all with black jackets and I don't have any money. I don't have anything. I don't know. Oh, oh, the eyes are there, always the eyes are there. Kind of covering me; I don't have to be afraid. Is there an accident down the road? What's the red, bright red.

Hypnotist: Bright red?

Barney Hill: Yeah, orange and red.

Hypnotist: Where is that?

Barney Hill: Right down the road.

Hypnotist: Down the road.

Barney Hill: I don't have to be afraid. But they won't talk to me.

Hypnotist: Who won't talk to you?

Barney Hill: The men.

Hypnotist: In the vehicle?

Barney Hill: No, there's standing in the road.

Hypnotist: And where are you? You're in the car?

Barney Hill: No, I'm just suspended. I'm just floating about. Oh, how funny. Just floating. I want to get back to the car but just floating about.

Hypnotist: You're really floating about or is that the way you feel.

Barney Hill: The way I feel.

Hypnotist: You're still outside of the car?

Barney Hill: No.

Hypnotist: You're in the car?

Barney Hill: I'm not in the car, I'm not *in* the car, I'm not in the woods, I'm not on the road.

Hypnotist: Well, where are these men?

Barney Hill: I don't know.

Hypnotist: On the road?

Barney Hill: I don't know, I'm just floating about. This is,... oh geez, that's the funniest thing Betty,...funniest thing. I never believed in flying saucers but; I don't know, not even mysteries, yeah, well, I guess won't say anything to anybody about this. It's too ridiculous isn't it. Yes it's funny, wonder where they came from. Oh geez I wish had gone with them...

Hypnotist: You wish you had gone with them?

Barney Hill: Yes. I would've experienced to go to some distant planet. Maybe this will prove the existence of God, isn't that funny. You look for the existence of God on other planets. Were you scared? I wasn't; … no I wasn't afraid. Anyways, wasn't anything anyways. It's ridiculous as I'm talking about it. I'll be getting into Portsmouth a little later than I expected.

Hypnotist: Alright we'll stop there. You'll be calm and relaxed. You will forget everything that we have had this period together until I ask you to recall it again. You will forget everything we have had now until I ask you to recall it again. You may wake now.

Wow! Two minutes after eight. Didn't you bring me in here ten minutes after eight?

Hypnotist: Yes.

Barney Hill: After ten. Where was I?

Hypnotist: Been right here.

Barney Hill: Where's my ciga...was I about to reach for a cigarette?

Hypnotist: Looked that way, go ahead and have one.

Barney Hill: I thought I was coming in here and you asked me to take this seat, this chair; and somehow I was reaching for a cigarette; but never reached for it.

Hypnotist: So how do you feel?

Barney Hill: I feel fine.

Hypnotist: Good. You know what happened here?

Barney Hill: I know you put me into a trance, I know the purpose of it but I don't...

Hypnotist: That's alright we'll continue this next week, a week from today.

***

Next session:

Hypnotist: What was it that you saw down the highway?

Barney Hill: I saw a group of men and they were standing in the highway and they came and they assisted me.

Hypnotist: Who assisted you?

Barney Hill: These men.

Hypnotist: They assisted you out of the car? That's what you said?

Barney Hill: Yes. I am only thinking of mental pictures as my eyes are closed and I think I am going up a slight incline and my feet are not bumping on the rocks. That's funny I thought of my feet bumping on the rocks and they are going up smoothly but I am afraid to open my eyes because I am being told strongly by myself to keep my eyes closed. Don't open them. And...I don't want to be operated on.

Hypnotist: You don't want to be operated on. What makes you think of an operation?

Barney Hill: I don't know.

Hypnotist: You were thinking about this when you were, when you were on the road?

Barney Hill: I was thinking about this when I was lying on my stomach.

Hypnotist: Where were you lying on your stomach?

Barney Hill: I...I thought I was inside something but I do not dare open my eyes. I had been told to keep my eyes closed.

Hypnotist: Who told you that?

Barney Hill: The... man.

Hypnotist: What man?

Barney Hill: That I saw through the binoculars.

Hypnotist: Was this one of the men in the road?

Barney Hill: No.

Hypnotist: Well who were these men in the road? What part did they play in this?

Barney Hill: They took me and carried me up this ramp.

Hypnotist: Did you feel you were going to be operated on?

Barney Hill: No.

Hypnotist: Did you feel you were going to be attacked in any way?

Barney Hill: No. I was laying on the table and my fly was open. And I thought 'are they putting a cup around my private parts?' And then it stopped and I thought, how funny.

Hypnotist: Speak a little louder please.

Barney Hill: I thought how funny; if I keep real quiet and real still I won't be harmed and it will be over and am walking and I walking...and, and being guided and my eyes are closed and I open my eyes and there is the car and the lights are off and it is not running and Delsey is under the seat and I reached under and touched her and she is in a tight ball under the seat and I sit back and I see Betty is coming down the road and she gets into the car and I am grinning at her and she is grinning back at me and we both seem so elated and we are really happy and I'm thinking it isn't too bad. How funny, I had no reason to fear and we look and I see a bright moon and I laugh and say, well there it goes. Ha, heh, and I'm happy.

End of transcript.

***

When the movie, 'The UFO Incident' came out in 1975 it was based on the actual recordings of the hypnosis sessions but a number of key details were left out. Of course they could not include the entire sessions; it would take too long and would likely have made for a boring movie. In particular one may notice that Barney Hill mentions that the 'men' he sees, one looks like a red-headed Irishmen and one looks like a Nazi. The movie does show James Earl Jones as Barney saying that one of them looks like a Nazi but he does not mention his comments that he thought he was being robbed; nor does it include this statement: "They're men; all with black jackets and I don't have any money..."

Here is a vintage photograph from the early 1960's that shows what some young bikers looked like in those days:

Notice the 'Nazi' symbols used, the 'duck-tail' haircuts and the black jackets. Under hypnosis Barney is clearly describing men, not aliens.

In the book 'Captured' by Stanton Friedman and Kathleen Marden[3], it is mentioned from one of Barney's hypnosis sessions that Barney gets nervous when he

---

[3] Captured! The Betty and Barney Hill UFO Experience: The True Story of the World's First Documented Alien Abduction page 94 (This book provides the most detailed and complete coverage of the Betty and Barney Hill Incident.)

sees men with duck-tail haircuts, suspecting they might be thugs. He anticipates hostility, but is relieved to find there is no hostility there.

Even the image that Barney drew under hypnosis is as follows:

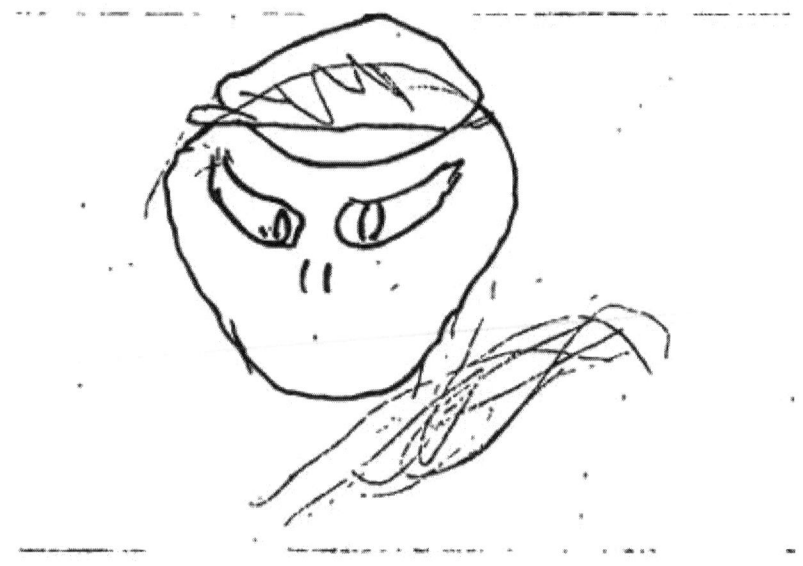

SKETCH OF "LEADER" DRAWN BY BARNEY HILL WHILE UNDER HYPNOSIS (COPY).

Barney described the men as follows:

"The figures, according to Barney Hill, were of human form dressed in shiny black uniforms and blade caps with peaks or bills on them (which could be seen when the figures turned their heads).

The uniforms were like glossy leather. (Under hypnosis, Mr. Hill said only the "leader" wore a shiny black coat or uniform and a peaked cap. The others wore light-colored shirts, similar to blue denim, and no caps.)"[4]

Again compare what Barney described to well known typical biker images:

---
[4] As reported by Walter Webb in his investigation from 1965.

Leather 'uniforms', caps and goggles. Suddenly the image of the leader alien that Barney drew under hypnosis does not look so alien anymore.

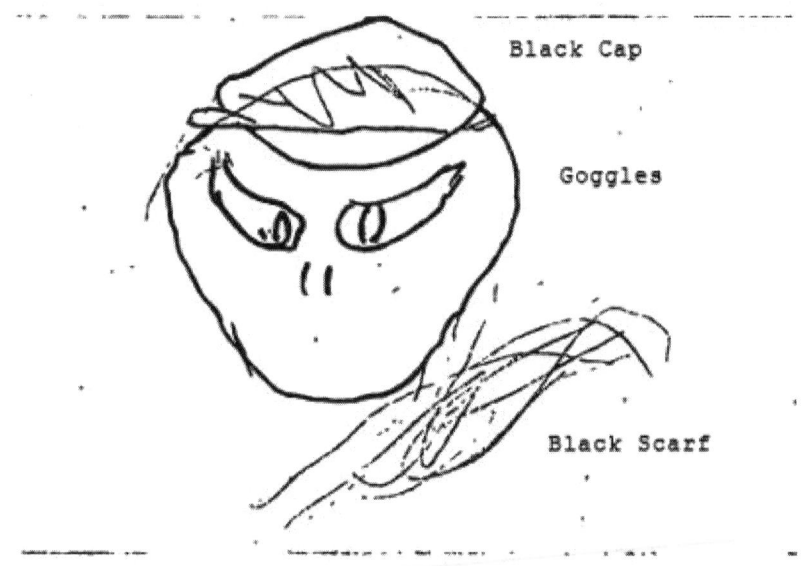

SKETCH OF "LEADER" DRAWN BY BARNEY HILL WHILE UNDER HYPNOSIS (COPY).

Also one must keep in mind that Barney actually served in World War II. He would have had many memories from that era as well. The black scarf, goggles and Nazi insignia were also common on German WWII pilots.

Barney also said under hypnosis that they assisted him. He says, "I saw a group of men and they were standing in the highway and they came and they assisted me". Why would he describe them as a group of men if he was experiencing an encounter with aliens?

In any case, one must remember that all these descriptions of the abduction are from the hypnosis sessions. The actual initial reports that they gave to the military were of them witnessing a UFO and had no mention whatsoever of being abducted. They did even mention seeing aliens at all. Betty later said that Barney did not want to be seen as a 'crackpot' if he told of seeing men in the UFO.

On September 26th, 1961 less than a week after her experience, Betty Hill wrote a letter to Major Donald Keyhoe.[5] She had just read his book 'The Flying saucer Conspiracy' and was very interested in getting more information about flying saucers. In her letter, she gives

---

[5] As reported by Walter Webb in his investigation from 1965.

an excellent description of her experience. Here is a transcription of that letter:

Dear Mr. Keyhoe:

The purpose of this letter is twofold. We wish to inquire if you have written any more books about unidentified flying objects since 'The Flying Saucer Conspiracy' was published.

If so, it would certainly be appreciated if you would send us the name of the publisher as we have been unsuccessful in finding any information more up to date than this book. A stamped self-addressed envelope is being included for your convenience.

My husband and I have become immensely interested in this topic, as we recently had quite a frightening experience, which does seem to differ from others of which we are aware. About midnight on September 20th, we were driving in a National Forest area in the White Mountain, in N.H. This is a desolate, uninhabited area. At first we notice a bright object in the sky which seemed to be moving rapidly. We stopped our car and got out to observe it more closely with our binoculars. Suddenly it reversed its flight from the north to the southwest and appeared to be flying in a very erratic pattern. As we continued driving and then stopping to watch it, we observed the following flight pattern.

The object was _spinning and appeared to be lighted only on one side which gave it a twinkling effect. As it approached our car, we stopped again. As it hovered in the air in front of us, it appeared to be pancake in shape, ringed.with windows in the front through which we could see bright blue-white lights. Suddenly two red lights appeared on each side. By this time my husband was standing in the road, watching closely';—He saw wings protrude on each side and the red lights were on the wing tips.

As it glided closer he was able to see inside this object, but not too closely. He did see many figures scurrying about, as though they were making some hurried type of preparation. One figure was observing us from the windows. From the distance, this was seen, the figures appeared to be about the size of a pencil, and seemed to be dressed in some type of shiny black uniform.

At this point, my husband became shocked and got back in the car, in a hysterical condition, laughing and repeating that they were going to capture us. He started driving the car - the motor had been left running. As we started to move, we heard several buzzing or beeping sounds which seemed to be striking the trunk of our car.

We did not observe this object leaving, but we did not see it again, although about thirty miles further south we were again bombarded by these same beeping sounds.

The next day we did make a report to an Air Force officer, who seemed to be very interested in the wings *and red lights. We did not report my husband's observation of the interior as it seems too fantastic to be true.*

At this time we are searching for any clue that might be helpful to my husband, in recalling whatever it was he saw that caused him to panic. His mind has completely blacked out at this point. Every attempt to recall, leaves him very frightened. We are considering the possibility of a competent psychiatrist who uses hypnotism.

This flying object was at least as large. as a four, motor, plane, its flight was noiseless and the lighting from the interior did not reflect on the grounds. There does not appear to be any damage to our car from the beeping sounds.

We both have been quite frightened by this experience, but fascinated. We feel a compelling urge to return to the spot where this occurred in the hope that we may again come in contact with this object. We realize this possibility is slight and we should, however, have more recent information regarding developments in the last six years.

Any suggested readings would be greatly appreciated. Your book has been of great help to us and a reassurance that we are not the only ones to have undergone an interesting and informative experience.

Very truly yours,

/s/ Mrs. Barney Hill

(Mrs.) Barney Hill

This letter that Betty wrote appears to be sincere and genuine with very little indications of embellishment or exaggeration. From my efforts at examining as much information as possible on this case, I would have to conclude that the Hills experienced an incident that closely matches the description that Betty Hill gave in the above letter. Unfortunately it appears that the hypnosis sessions opened up a large volume of what I can best describe as 'scrambled' memories.

The second factor that scrambled, obfuscated or other wise muddied the eventual re-telling of their incident is the fact that as time progressed, the details of their experience kept growing larger and more and more incredible. Unfortunately Barney Hill passed away quite young, aged 46 in 1969; but Betty lived to age 85 and passed away in 2004. It appears that she added many more details over time that may have been a combination of altered memories and subjective mis-interpretations of various events. This can be seen in the rare interview she did in October of 1999; the transcript of which, never before published, I've included in here:

A Rare Interview of Betty Hill in 1999:

Interviewer: We're talking with Betty Hill, famous and first abductee. September 19th, 1961, Betty while driving with her husband Barney, was heading south from Canada...

Betty Hill: Right.

Interviewer: ...when very early in the morning, you saw a strange light behind the car. It was September 19. What time was that Betty when this light behind the car appeared?

Betty Hill: Well, we crossed over the border into New Hampshire and I think we started to see the lights following actually in the very beginning I noticed a bright light in the sky and I thought I was discovering a new planet; until it started to move. And this was about 10:30, 11 o'clock at night. So we stopped the car and got out to see what this, we thought it was a flight. We stopped the car and got out to look at it and that's when it changed direction and started coming in towards us. Now that about the Lancaster area; and then it followed us for about thirty miles; chased our car.

Interviewer: And all the while you were discussing it, 'what is this? What is that?'

Betty Hill: Yes, Barney was trying to, he knew planes, he was trying to identify it. And it's flying in a very erratic manner. This is very strange for us, but this is '61. We could UFO but actually in those days we called them flying saucers. We had no idea what a flying saucer looked like but we were, we had no fear, just curiosity, we were trying to identify this craft.

Interviewer: You go on in the road, you decide to pull over, Barney gets out of the car...

Betty Hill: Actually that was in the Indian Head area.

Interviewer: Okay, am I preceding something here when you encountered alien entities or was this after.

Betty Hill: This is the next step.

Interviewer: Okay.

Betty Hill: In the Indian Head area, I'm trying to attract the attention of this craft, I'm going, 'c'mon in, Hi,'...I got the window down, I'm yelling, 'Hi ho, who are you?' At that point, it left the top of the mountain, came out over the highway and stopped in mid-air directly in front of us; maybe about fifty feet in the sky. So Barney got out with the binoculars in an attempt to identify the craft. And when he looked up he saw a circular window with a bright light behind it and he saw these men standing behind the window looking down at him. And at that point, the craft began to descend and he became frightened. Ran back to the car saying he thought they were trying to capture him.

So we got in the car and went speeding down the highway to avoid capture. And as we're driving along there's beeping sounds; sounds like something was hitting the trunk of the car and the car vibrated. Then we drove along for about another thirty miles and Barney turned off onto a side road. And here were the group of men we seen on the craft; standing in the middle of the road walking our way and naturally we had to start our car. And they came up in two groups, took us out of the car, passed into the woods to where the craft was one the ground.

Interviewer: At that point, strange thoughts started going through your head; thoughts that weren't your own. Did you have some sort of telepathic communication with these entities or…

Betty Hill: All our communication was verbal.

Interviewer: Verbal?

Betty Hill: Right.

Interviewer: Oh, interesting.

Betty Hill: Yup, they spoke English in a limited way, like a foreigner coming here and not too well acquainted with our language.

Interviewer: But at the same time using common colloquialisms of the day like, 'You'll be back in no time' or something of that ilk.

Betty Hill: Yeah, uh, you know, in the very first part they had us under some kind of control and I brought myself out of this but Barney was only able to bring himself out, partly out of it; so I was just as conscious as I am right now.

Interviewer: They walk you into the craft up a ramp. The landed craft, this is right off route 3…, well actually you didn't know where you were at that point.

Betty Hill: Uh yeah, right off route 3.

Interviewer: So they walk you up this ramp, you're brought in and what did they say you were going to do with you?

Betty Hill: well, when we got to the door, I was not going to go in so I punched him.

Interviewer: You punched the entity?

Betty Hill: Yeah, in fact I put such a battle that my dress was badly torn. And he said, 'come on, all we want to do is a simple test, as soon as the tests are over you can go back to your car and you'll be on your way'.

Interviewer: Let's just go back to those type of entities, they were you're classic alien grey shaped…

Betty Hill: No…

Interviewer: No, no they weren't...

Betty Hill: They were a form of human beings.

Interviewer: They were a form of human beings. Did they have cat-like or chesire like eyes?

Betty Hill: They had larger eyes than ours, small nose, small mouth, no protruding part of the ear and no hair. They were people.

Interviewer: Nothing like these classic greys you see...

Betty Hill: I've never seen those.

Interviewer: Okay, there was a leader.

Betty Hill: We gave them different names to identify them. Now I don't know if he was the leader or the interpreter, but we called him the leader. Then the one who did the testing, we called him the examiner. There were nine others who stayed out in the corridor and we called them the crew members.

Interviewer: Okay, so you're on board. What, do you remember what you saw when you entered the craft. Something must have taken you aback, saying, 'this is amazing' or 'what type of craft am I inside'. Can you describe as to what you collectively remember?

Betty Hill: Went in to a corridor and then I was taken into a room and I had to step up because the floor, the level of the floor was above the corridor and it was an oval shaped door like we would see on a ship.

Interviewer: Do you remember at that point; did they specify their agenda at that point? Were you going in immediately for the examination or...

Betty Hill: They were taking us strictly to; actually they wanted to find out how we were like them or different from them, physically.

Interviewer: Did you feel that you were chosen for this or that you happen to be in the wrong area at the wrong time? Or the right area at the right time?

Betty Hill: Well, now I figure it was the right time and the right area; but I think we, I brought it on myself you know I was waving to them and yelling to them, and 'who are you?' and all.

Interviewer: You get into the examination room, you're separated from Barney.

Betty Hill: Right. They take him into the second room.

Interviewer: Your examination, and again all this comes out in later dreams and hypnosis but immediately do they remove your clothes and perform, what happens? You'll have to; I'm tainted by all the popular lore of abduction stories.

Betty Hill: I don't know anything about those stories.

Interviewer: That's good, you're better off.

Betty Hill: But ah, I was taken into this first room and uh, it was quite bare, there was a small table, a stool and then the wall, there were doors on the wall that would slide back and forth and they put me on the stool checked my eyes, ears, nose, throat, my feet, my hands and then they put me on a table, said they were gonna check my nervous system. And they used some kind of equipment to do this. And then he tried to insert a needle-like instrument in my navel which caused me pain so they stopped doing it. And, uh, then the examiner left, went into the room where Barney was.

Interviewer: Can you describe what was happening to Barney? What Barney recalled under hypnosis some, what was going on at the same time in his examination room?

Betty Hill: Uh, with Barney most of the exam was the same except uh they were interested in his bone structure and they were feeling all up and down his spine, his arms and all, basically.

Interviewer: Did Barney recall any struggle akin to the struggle you had?

Betty Hill: No. They had him under this control, he had uh, it was very upsetting to him because he couldn't move.

Interviewer: So he, they had implemented paralysis, some sort of temporary paralysis on Barney to subdue him whereas to you they gave you a little more leeway as far as you weren't...

Betty Hill: Well I'm small. I was smaller than them so I didn't get a big dose of paralysis.

Interviewer: So they saw him as more of a fear perhaps.

Betty Hill: He was bigger than them, taller.

Interviewer: Okay. Your examination concludes, then what happens?

Betty Hill: Well, while the examiner is in doing Barney's exam, I started talking with the leader and I said, "I know you're not from this planet, where are you from?" And he showed me a star map and he explained part of it, the map to me briefly um and then we just talked about food and different aspects of life here.

Interviewer: And then what? Give me some...

Betty Hill: Actually what led to food was the examiner came running back in the room where I was and started tugging at my teeth. And (chuckle) he wanted to know why Barney's teeth were removable and mine were not.

Interviewer: And the story is Barney had dentures?

Betty Hill: Yup, during World War Two, Barney got too close to a hand grenade; knocked his teeth out.

Interviewer: And they were totally confused by all this.

Betty Hill: That was very puzzling to them.

Interviewer: And humorous. Any other instances of something as a human you took so general as a characteristic that you never thought of it that they got confused by; almost child-like you know akin to the denture incident? Was there anything else like that, that they seemed; boy you don't know that? That you can recall?

Betty Hill: Well I was sort of disappointed, I didn't know anything about their solar system. I think they really expected me to be able to identify the map.

Interviewer: They were actually upset that you didn't recognize their home. Let's go to that Marjorie Fish months later or years later actually, under hypnosis. Tries to induce you under hypnosis to re-draw that star map.

Betty Hill: Nope, no, no, no.

Interviewer: Okay, maybe you can go over that.

Betty Hill: Dr. Simon, at the time, Benjamin Simon, said that during the week, if I wanted to I would be able to remember the star map; and I would sketch it. But I was not to think, it was just my hand would go ahead and draw it; which I did. And that was in 1965.

Interviewer: Four years after the incident.

Betty Hill: Yeah, now in 1969 Marjorie Fish came here and stayed for a few days; asked me all kinds of questions; hours and hours, which he taped. And then used that to go back home and did the research on it and identified the areas.

Interviewer: The area of the star map which she said was in the constellation which we know Reticulus and the star system was Zeta Reticuli and from that point do you remember them mentioning Zeta Reticuli terminology or was that something we as Earthlings have given them.

Betty Hill: I would have no idea what they may have termed their home planet.

Interviewer: Do you remember what type of star system? Was it a white star, yellow star, red giant or do you recall what type of star or anything?

Betty Hill: I don't know, but I do know that astronomers believe that the stars on my map were the ones most likely to have life; to have planets and have life.

Interviewer: And they may be younger stars? Hotter stars.

Betty Hill: Actually, we're believed to between four and six billion years old.

Interviewer: Or twenty billion, it seems we age a billion years every five years, so…

Betty Hill: But actually Zeta Reticuli, we believe, we don't know for sure, we believe is about eleven billion years old. They've been around a lot longer than we have.

Interviewer: Twice, over twice as long and the chance to 'evolutionize', to …so this puzzling incident, you're examined, you get a tour of the space ship or the craft or anything, or it's only on a need to know basis?

Betty Hill: No, just one room I was in.

Interviewer: The interaction with you and the question answer session was more than Barney; they did not give Barney the opportunity to inquire.

Betty Hill: No, no, there was no conversation with Barney. I enjoyed myself, I had a good time. He joked, we kidded.

Interviewer: Really.

Betty Hill: Yup, I invited him to come back, I said, "please, please, please come back, oh I have so many friends who would love to meet you."

Interviewer: It was not a traumatic experience at all.

Betty Hill: No.

Interviewer: It was an enlightening experience. Spiritually uplifting perhaps.

Betty Hill: Right; nobody can tell me there's not life on other planets.(laughs)

Interviewer: At the same time, it seems that thirty-six hours after the sighting; it is on record, according to Jacques Vallee, at 2:14 AM Pease Air Force was tracking an unknown object.

Betty Hill: Oh yeah, I told him that. Pease Air Force Base released the radar report where they tracked this craft, sent two planes out to check it out and the reports of the pilots are still classified so we know what chumps they are.

Interviewer: To the skeptic, it kind of knocks them out of the water if; for you to guess this concocted story; you really know your stuff or it's a pretty well orchestrated event to have Pease personnel involved and to say that Betty and Barney you know, Barney was a postal worker?

Betty Hill: Yeaup.

Interviewer: A postal worker, you're involved in real estate and that you pulled off a grand hoax through the air force; it's nearly impossible if not impossible; absurd I guess is the term I'm looking for. You're released from the craft, you get back into the car, you check your watches, why?

Betty Hill: Well, I don't think we checked our watches until we were almost home, we wanted to know what time it was and both our watches had stopped functioning.

Interviewer: And you could not account for some time elapsed?

Betty Hill: We realized the trip had taken much longer than it should have; maybe about two hours.

Interviewer: Were you feeling woozy, did you have a headache, did you have any physical, were you just exhausted, what were, can you describe what your feeling was?

Betty Hill: We'd been driving all night, we got home about five in the morning; we were calm, relaxed, feeling very well.

Interviewer: So you didn't feel traumatized or injured at any time?

Betty Hill: No.

Interviewer: Or should I say violated at that time?

Betty Hill: (shakes her head no)

Interviewer: You go in the house, the next morning, you check out the car and what happens when you look at the car?

Betty Hill: Clearly polished spots on the trunk of the car. And that day it was really getting tropical rain from a hurricane that was going through; and a heavy downpour and it didn't affect the spots at all. They stayed there for months.

Interviewer: Your sister, who claimed to have seen a UFO suggested that you do what? Around the car?

Betty Hill: Oh, that was a physicist who said go out with a compass and check out those spots which we did.

Interviewer: What happened?

Betty Hill: and the compass was very, very erratic.

Interviewer: Was spinning?

Betty Hill: Yeah, (makes circular back and forth hand gesture), we tried it on different other parts of the car and it didn't react that way.

Interviewer: But just near where the spots were?

Betty Hill: Yes. That's right.

Interviewer: The inference being a magnetic anomaly, something was really distorting the magnetic draw of the compass. At that point, afterwards, you contact CUFO's J Allen...

Betty Hill: No.

Interviewer: What is the sequence of events?

Betty Hill: First of all we didn't do anything. And then at NICAP in Washington, I wrote to them because I wanted to know being exposed to a UFO, close range, were there any health problems? Exposed to radiation, what kind of dangers?

Interviewer: They dispatched Walter Webb as their representative. That leeter winds up with NICAP and the Centre for UFO studies, Dr. J. Allen Hynek.

Betty Hill: It might have, I don't know.

Interviewer: You never, ever communicated with Dr. Hynek?

Betty Hill: Oh no, we did. We were good friends, well that was years later. We did numerous TV programs together.

Interviewer: What was your feeling on Dr. Hynek, was he obviously a thinly veiled skeptic?

Betty Hill: Oh no, no, no. He believed every word of it.

Interviewer: At the end.

Betty Hill: As soon as he met ud.

Interviewer: It seems his take on the UFO phenomena when he was humiliated with the 'swamp gas' incident, to draw out an absurd explanation in front of a college dorm I believe in Michigan, the Great Lakes, that's when he said enough, the government was masquerading or at least trotting out disinformation and misinformation on UFO phenomena.

Betty Hill: Of course when he pressed that, he was working for the government.

Interviewer: So Dr. Hynek and you were great friends then.

Betty Hill: Oh yeah. Yup, and his son lived down here in Massachusetts.

Interviewer: So you're having some trouble in dreams now; what happens at home.

Betty Hill: Actually, ten nights after this happened, I had a series of dreams; five nights, **each dream was different which later I found out was a recall of what had happened.**

Interviewer: In the dreams you were depicting what you just described to me?

Betty Hill: (Nodding yes) Yup.

Interviewer: At that point what do you do? Is Barney having trouble with this? Is Barney, has his life pattern changed?

Betty Hill: No.

Interviewer: Has his mood changed at all.

Betty Hill: Actually, the first thing I did was, during the next day, I wrote down what I could remember of my dreams.

Interviewer: The following day which would be the twentieth.

Betty Hill: And every time, no it was ten nights after.

Interviewer: So we're talking the 20th and 30th roughly.

Betty Hill: Yeah, and I wrote, I made a record.

Interviewer: Thirty-eight years to the day.

Betty Hill: And then I took and put them away. And then later, several months later I talked with my supervisor about the meaning of dreams and she said, "Well, maybe it happened."

Interviewer: And suggested or…

Betty Hill: We just talked about it.

***

You can clearly see how Betty's interpretation of the events from 38 years earlier have changed drastically from her original impressions that she expressed to Donald Keyhoe one week after the incident. (The balance of her 1999 interview can be found in the appendix.)

The extreme change in a first hand account is something that is not uncommon; the recall that we have of childhood traumatic events has a tendency to change over time and a person is sometimes shocked to see how different their memory is of an event compared to that of their parents of grandparents. Combine the passage of time with in-depth hypnosis plus the subjective interpretation of dreams and you have a recipe for even more confusion and aberrations. How often does a person dream of things that turn out to be actual events that have been somehow consciously forgotten? I know most of my dreams are nothing more than a combination of fantasy, snippets of real life events and indirect reflections of personal life experiences but that's just me.

In spite of Betty's morphed storytelling over time and in spite of the huge of coverage of this case, both positive and negative, it remains as one the most pivotal and groundbreaking events in the history of Alien Abduction research.

Chapter 2 - Financial Considerations

Another one of the most famous alien abduction events ever recorded happened in Arizona on November 5th in 1975. Travis Walton, Mike Rogers and five other lumberjacks were driving home through the forest when they saw what they thought was a UFO through the trees. A public documentary of the case produced these details:

Travis Walton:

"Well, as I stopped the truck there... The guys were yelling at me to stop the truck. They'd seen something off to the right there, clearly after we'd broke through a group of pine trees there. We looked over to our right and there hovering above the ground twenty feet or so, above the ground and about one hundred feet from the truck was a large glowing object."

Travis had jumped out of the truck and had gone forward and started walking right up underneath it.

Travis Walton:

"I was just thinking that this thing was just gonna take off and it would be gone before I got up close. I was pretty scared myself and I made up my mind to make a run for it and when I raised up 'Wham!' Something hit me, just like a physical blow, it was kind of a tingling, shocking sort of feeling and I just blacked out."

Mike Rogers: "I jerked my head back around to see what the source of the light was and here's Travis flying back through the air. He landed some distance from where he'd been standing. He landed flat on his back. The guys in the back seat were yelling at me to get the hell out of there and I hit the gas and we were gone down the road."

According to Travis, the next thing he remembers was waking up in what he describes as a large dark room, laying on a cold metal platform, surrounded by alien creatures.

Travis Walton:

"I was definitely not in a hospital."

Interviewer: Can you describe what these aliens looked like?

"Well, they were basically humanoid, you know, two arms, two legs, like that, but they had very large heads, no hair, sort of a pale grayish-white skin."

He says that he remembered a large surgical instrument being lowered down onto him and used to remove fluid from his eyes. Within days of his disappearance, Travis Walton's story hit the headlines across America. Despite an extensive search in the forest, no one could find any evidence of what happened.

The police believe that the group might have murdered Travis and disposed of the body. But Mike and the others all passed polygraph tests and stuck to their UFO story.

Interviewer: You and the other lads in the truck were convinced that you'd seen a UFO and it had taken Travis.

Mike Rogers: "We weren't convinced that we had seen a UFO, we were absolutely positive that we had seen a UFO. It wasn't just a UFO, an Unidentified Flying Object; this was a definite flying object. It was very close, very vivid and burn edged in my memory forever."

And then, just as mysteriously as he'd left, Travis woke up on the outskirts of town, just a short distance from where the UFO had been. He was dazed and disorientated.

Interviewer: How long were you actually gone for?

"I was missing for five days and six hours and some odd minutes. Although the night I was returned I was under the impression it had just been a short while, I thought it was the same night."

Travis and the other six men underwent an intensive battery of tests and examinations by experts. As crazy as their story was, no one was able to prove a hoax or a fraud.

Travis Walton: "What we saw, was not that far away. I mean, we could see that thing. It was clear, it was distinct. It wasn't just a point of light in the sky or anything like this. This was very close. We could have thrown a rock and hit it. I was scared but like everyone there I got out and went towards it. It might have been a foolish thing but I was thinking this thing might take off, you know. I just wanted to get a closer look and figured it would vanish. "

Mike Rogers: "After we put maybe a quarter mile distance between us and it, I suddenly realized what we had done and I realized that our friend was back there and I had left him there. So, I stopped the truck. Several of us didn't want that at all. I said well, we have to, we have to go back. He could be hurt. Obviously he is hurt. And we can help him. We went back to the site, that thing was gone, Travis was gone. So, we thought maybe he wandered off somewhere. So we conducted a hand-in-hand search you might say, six grown men walking around the woods, about as close to each other as they could get. We decided that we haven't been able to find him. If we would have to do something, what could we do? All we could think was to go to the authorities."

The Sheriff arrived and listened to their story. He was cautious but not completely disbelieving. He decided the only thing to do was to go back up the hill in the morning and look for Travis.

Mike Rogers: "Three of the guys had no intention to go back to the hill. They wanted to stay right back there where they were. And so me and one other fella and several of the Sheriff people went back up the hill and covered all the roads below and above and we looked for tracks, we looked for signs. We listened; we couldn't find him at all. There was no trace of him at all, no tracks of any kind anywhere. It just seemed that that thing must have taken him; whoever they were we had no idea at that point. Somebody from, somewhere else in this world, had taken him and he was just not there."

Mike Rogers and the Sheriff went to inform Walton's mother that their son was missing.

Mike Rogers: "All through that night and for the next several days it was incomprehensible. We, we could not understand what had happened. It just didn't sink in. Something had happened, something odd had happened. We did not know if it was terrible, whether it was great. We didn't know, but it was something that we could not understand that had happened and that was, it was very traumatic, very traumatic, the most traumatic event that I have ever encountered."

The Sheriff from Holbrook expected that the men had murdered Travis and buried his body in the woods. And that they were using the UFO story as an alibi.

A few days later, the polygraph examiner gave an official report. They told Mike Rogers that this was the first time that the polygraph examiner had such a large number subjects regarding the same event. He said that his findings positively proved the men did see something they believed to be a UFO.

Travis Walton: "When I felt the numbing shock, I blacked out, and the next thing I knew, I regained consciousness. Not quickly, sort of gradually. My head wasn't real clear. I was in a lot of pain. I was laying on my back. I did not know where I was. I... I remembered what had happened in the woods. As I was regaining consciousness, I was trying to figure out what it was and what was going on. Maybe I was in a hospital or something as I had been hurt.

I was standing in front of those things which were coming towards me and they stopped there and stood there looking at me. These huge eyes just seemed to, just looked right through me. I did not get any impression of emotion, it was very detached, sort of just observance. It seemed like they could see everything I was thinking and dreaming. Very disturbing feeling to feel so exposed. These huge eyes looked at me and when they blink and on an eye that big eyelids would just slid down and open like a, like a window, opening and shutting and it was just, I had the strangest sort of feeling. I just couldn't, I couldn't bear their gaze."

"There was a lever there. And when I moved that, the star pattern began to move. That kind of disorientated me for a minute because you know, it felt like I was moving for a second because this was, you know, everything suddenly shifted like that. But I figured out that I better quit messing with that and, you know, by that time I surmised that I was in some sort of craft and connected to what had happened before figured out that I might crash this thing or something. This person was not like the humanoid creatures that I had seen before. This looked like a human being, like a man, in a blue uniform. I went up to him thinking you know I was being rescued, that I was being saved. That this was a person you know. I started asking all kinds of questions, like: "Where am I? You were out. Who are those these that I saw? Talk to me! He took me through some doors down the hallway to another room."

Five days had passed before Travis returned. He was asked to take a lie detector test. He too passed. Little did he know that this event would cast a shadow over the rest of his life.

Travis: "The thing that has brought more frustration and pain in my life as a result of all this happening is the fact that people can't see me anymore. Me as a person. I get a feeling of invisibility, because of this thing. Every contact I have with people, is covered by, is filtered through the distorting lens of something that just happened to me, 50 years ago. And it is something that just happened to me. I didn't do anything special or heroic. I am not a hero or a celebrity any more than I am a disceiving rascal or… or a crack pot space cadet sort of person. I would just like to be seen as myself rather than in terms this thing that just happened to me. It could have happened to anyone."

Stanton Friedman (UFO Researcher): "Well, I spent a day with Travis and Mike Rogers. He passed the lie detector test. Their story is consistent. There were five other people there after all who saw all of these events unfold. They've also passed the lie detector test. His story is consistent. It's never changed. I've found his story profoundly convincing."

So what did happen to Travis Walton that night in 1975? What did he and the other loggers see in the forest? Where did Travis disappear to for five days?

Interviewer: What do you say to people who say, you know, these seven guys just made this whole story up?

"Ha! I mean... you know, seven people are saying the same thing, they stick by their stories for over two decades. You know, all of us have taken polygraph tests; more than one polygraph test. Every theory the skeptics come up with is just absurd, I mean, easily proven so."

There was another interesting fact that wasn't reported at the time. A radiation test was done on the clothes and hats that the group were wearing on the night. The Geiger counter gave an abnormally high reading, a six on a scale of ten. If this was all a hoax or some sort of mass delusion, where did this high level of radiation come from?

Stanton Friedman: "I'm absolutely convinced that Travis Walton was indeed abducted. Their stories are consistent. I've listened to the objections of the noisy negativists about this story, and as is almost always the case they don't stand up. Once you check on them and don't accept them blindly.

I'm convinced he's telling the truth along with Mike because of all this peripheral stuff, the polygraphs, etc."

***

To read this documented account and to watch the coverage portrayed in the many 'made-for-TV' documentaries, it is easy to get a strong sense that the incident is cut and dried and really happened as described; yet upon closer examination, the Travis Walton incident is as far from clear as mud is from water.

This incident has produced hundreds of pages of documented evidence. It took me days to go over all the details from many sources — and this brings up a very real problem in examining cases of Alien Abduction; the amount of information and analysis just keeps growing and growing over time.

A large part of the evidence consists of the efforts of Philip J. Klass, who seemed to work tirelessly at attacking the character and credibility of Mike Rogers. Philip Klass passed away in 2005 and although he had a high level of skepticism on the subject of UFOs, he would sometimes resort to character attacks (ad hominem arguments) when corresponding with people. His harsh analysis did not win him many friends.

After going through all the evidence I could find and then trying to digest it all, there were a number of things that seemed to leave a lasting impression. A lot of the argumentative correspondence seems to fade away but these three points stand out.

First is the story from the National Enquirer that includes a photo of Travis Walton holding up a check for $2,500. Was there a financial incentive for these men to fabricate a story? Klass dug up all sorts of nasty details on how Mike Rogers was having difficulty with his obligations to the government for lumber work and how he may have been under pressure from these obligations to not be completely forthright in his business dealings. Past legal events involving fraud also came to light but let's give these men the benefit of a doubt. Maligning a person's character is not really helpful when searching for facts; it can raise suspicions of course but let's just assume that these men were all average, upstanding, decent guys. The National Enquirer would run a contest every year and award $5000 to $10,000 for the best UFO incident of the year. The contest eventually offered up to $100,000 if a case was provided that 'proved' alien visitation. What better way to prove alien visitation than by being abducted by one?

    The men involved met with the Enquirer soon after the incident and the story was announced in the December 16th, 1975 issue and then the story of them getting the $5,000 reward was shown in the July 13th, 1976 issue.

It is impossible to tell whether the men were aware of the reward before the incident occurred. The National Enquirer had a very large circulation; whether it would be 'common knowledge' for most folks to be aware of the potential for a 'big payoff' with an astounding UFO story; I could only guess, most likely it would indeed be common knowledge.

Second is the polygraph test that was conducted by John McCarthy. This was required by the National Enquirer to be eligible for the prize money. If money was an incentive, then Travis Walton would have wanted to take and pass this test as soon as possible. (Strangely enough, it was not actually the first polygraph that was conducted – see appendix for details on the first test that was passed) The test was conducted just ten days after the initial incident and just five days after Travis Walton was found, that is, after having been missing for five days, it was another five when he took the test. There was certainly very little time wasted from the moment he was found to the time of discussing with the paper about being eligible for the prize money. Here is a transcript of that polygraph report:

16 November 1975

RE: WALTON, TRAVIS C.

On 15 November, Travis C. WALTON was given a polygraph examination for The National Enquirer, at the request of Mr. Paul JENKINS, reference WALTON'S recent UFO experience. The examination commenced at 1425 and was. concluded at 1615 hours.

During the examination, he showed gross deception on the charts,as he answered the following relevant questions as Indicated:
Were you actually taken aboard a spacecraft near Hober on November 5th? ... "Yes"
Were you actually in a spacecraft from the 5th to the 10th of November? ... "Yes".

Have you lied to Dr. HARDER about being in a spacecraft? ... "No".

Have you acted in collusion with others to perpetrate a UFO hoax? ... "No".

Did you lie to any of sheriff GILLESPIE'S questions concerning your disappearance? ... "No"

Were you hiding somewhere in Arizona during your disappearance?
No"

Have you been advised by anyone to lie on this examination? "... "No"

His reactions on the control test were normal. He appeared to be lucid, and prior to testing stated that he understood each of the questions to be asked, and that he could answer each with a "Yes" or "No".

It was obvious during the examination that he was deliberately attempting to distort his respiration pattern.

Based on his reactions on all charts, it is the opinion of this examiner that WALTON, in concert with others, is attempting to perpetrate a UFO hoax, and that he has not been on any spacecraft.

JOHN J. MCCARTHY
Examiner

Whether The Enquirer approached Travis Walton first or not is not very relevant but the fact that they did meet just a few days after the incident is; the evidence of such a meeting negates any comments from the individuals involved that may have indicated that they did not want to have any media exposure. The Polygraph Examiner was under agreement to keep the results secret but he later released the results because he felt that the knowledge of the test was already released[6] and he was trying to prevent a hoax. After this, McCarthy was attacked in various reports, the test results were disputed, further polygraph tests (as well as the prior) were done by other examiners which were passed and on and on. Yet, this particular test remains as a very significant thorn in the overall story.

---

[6] See additional John McCarthy transcript in Appendix 2.

Lastly there is the case of the interviews conducted prior to Travis Walton being found. While a search was being conducted for Travis Walton on the evening of November 8th, 1975 a fellow by the name of Fred Sylvanus, (he was head of Arizona Regional UFO Project and a member of Ground Saucer Watch) conducted an interview with Mike Rogers and Duane Walton (Travis' step brother). Here is a partial transcript of the interview between Fred and Duane:

Duane: "I don't believe he's hurt or injured in any way. He will be back sooner or later, whenever they get done what they're doing."

Sylvanus: You feel he will come back?

Duane: "Sure do. Don't feel any fear for him at all. Little regret because
I haven't been able to experience the same thing. That's about it."

Sylvanus: You feel you just miss him and he'll come back?
Duane: "He's not even missing. He knows where he's at and I know where he's at."

Sylvanus: You know where he's at?
Duane: "Basically, he's not in the woods. They took him for whatever purpose they take people, to run a few tests."

Sylvanus: Well, where do you feel he is?
Duane: "Not on this earth."
(Later in the interview)

Sylvanus: You know that he's going to come back?
Duane: "Sure do. It's a matter of time. They don't kill people."

Sylvanus: You feel that he'll be found?
Duane: "Yeah, he'll be found and if he doesn't come back, it'll be voluntary because he wanted to stay."

This is really a case of letting the cat out the bag. Duane is stating that he knows where Travis is and that he will be found two days prior to him actually showing up again. A member of the Travis Walton family or a close friend must have let Duane in on what was going on so that he would not have to go through unnecessary agony at the loss of Travis.

Those are the three main points that seem to nail the coffin shut on this particular incident. There are many, many more details of information about this case and a lot of it is conflicting and contradictory. The main point I would like to express is that this incident is not the same as what is portrayed on so many made for TV documentaries that just swallow the main story as a cut-and-dried verified event that happened exactly as the lumbermen describe. This case, similar to the Betty and Barney Hill Incident, was made into a book and movie and became a part of the typical Alien Abduction phenomenon. On a side note it is interesting to know that the made-for-TV movie about Betty and Barney Hill aired on television on October 20th, 1975, just sixteen days before the Travis Walton incident.

If a jury of twelve people examined all the evidence in this case would they feel that the experience of Travis Walton was genuine or a hoax? I think if the jury was made up of suspicious skeptics then of course they would immediately call it a hoax but if the jury was made up of average folks, I think it would be a hung jury; that is, it would be hard to get twelve people to agree definitely one way or the other. All of the evidence that is available on the case does not contribute towards an iron-clad case of proven alien abduction; on the contrary it paints a picture of mostly circumstantial evidence that tilts the history of the event dangerously close to the precipice of a money motivated hoax. The reader will be left to confirm these details and make up their own mind.

    I believe the Travis Walton case is similar to the pain and anguish that Betty and Barney Hill experienced. Travis Walton and the lumber men experienced a painful, life altering event; he is a victim. The reality of the event is clear in his own mind and that is all that matters as far as the quality of *his* life is concerned. It is only natural that he would be interested in financial compensation for the psychological torture he has been through both from the event and the mental turmoil of having to deal with it afterwards, essentially for the rest of his life.

Similar to the Betty and Barney Hill case, the initial view of the UFO should be kept separate from the specific abduction details. The initial view of the UFO seems genuine but the abduction story may have been unintentionally embellished due to trauma, post-traumatic stress, hypnosis implications, injury or debilitating nightmares leading to altered memories of the event.

The genuineness of the actual event itself becomes less important when you realize the individuals involved are often subject to ridicule and persecution and who need the support and care of their community to get back to a normal productive life.

Chapter 3 - Dreaming of Aliens

After the airing of 'The UFO Incident' in 1975 and the widespread press coverage of the Travis Walton incident over the following year, the number of cases of Alien Abduction exploded. The debate about whether alien abductions are real has raged on since then for decades. For abductees, the experiences are vivid and frightening events, many with physical interaction with aliens and spacecraft. But some skeptics say that what they are really experiencing is a form of severe sleep disorder.

Dr. Susan Blackmore (Psychologist at the University of Plymouth): "The more I hear about abduction stories, particularly the ones that happen in bed, at night, when people are asleep, the more I can see the similarities between that and what's called sleep paralysis. Sleep paralysis is surprisingly common. Something like 30 per cent of people have it. When you are dreaming you have to be paralyzed, but normally that wears off long before you ever wake up, so you don't know anything about it. But sometimes the mechanism goes wrong so that you wake up and you're still paralyzed.

This paralysis is very often associated with buzzing and humming noises, feelings of floating or flying up or being dragged away, creepy crawly skin sensations, as there's something running up and down your skin, and overwhelming all of that a sense of presence, the feeling that there's somebody there in the room with you.

And when it wears off, you just… if you don't know what it is it can be pretty frightening. Now, you can see the many similarities between that and alien abductions. I think a lot of alien abductions accounts are in fact elaborations of sleep paralysis."

Yvonne Smith (Alien Abductee Researcher): "But we know for a fact that not all of these abductees are sleeping. And they're having these experiences. Yes, there is sleep paralysis and yes, if they're asleep maybe part of that could be sleep paralysis. But when a person is sitting up in bed reading and a bright light floods the room and they become paralyzed and can't move and they feel something is in their room, how do you explain that? How do you explain people driving on a highway? They're not asleep and they're not always by themselves, so they're not making this up because they have witnesses."

Dr. David Jacobs (Temple University): "This (has always been considered) inherently unbelievable. This is the fringe of the fringe. People are telling us that they're being abducted by aliens from another planet. This is (considered) prima facie evidence of mental instability and has been for many, many years.

For the first 20 or 30 years of this phenomenon, all we did was try to research what were the psychological and psychiatric reasons for why this could be happening. We've got to find the reasons for it because it's obviously psychological. It can't be happening the way people are describing it.

Well, it's not psychological. And it's not psychiatric. And it is happening, I think by and large, the way people are describing it. And **I think that what we're looking at here is a physiological program of exploitation by one species of another.**"

Furthermore it is quite clear that Dr. Blackmore's assumptions or theory of explanation can really only be applied to cases where the individuals in question were sleeping or in bed. Her argument provides no explanation for those abduction cases that occur while driving down a road or walking in the woods, or any situation other than in one's bedroom.

On the other hand, Michael Raduga is the founder and the head of the OOBE (Out of Body Experience) Research Center. He has conducted experiments at UCLA (University of California at Los Angeles) dealing with Alien Encounters in a dream like or lucid dream state. He concludes:

"The majority of subjects underwent at least one full or partial out-of-body experience, while some experienced several. Subjects who became conscious while dreaming were instructed to transform the "lucid dream" into an out-of-body experience by returning to the physical body in order to separate from it.

The fact that UFOs and extraterrestrials may be deliberately encountered in a controlled manner and within a few days proves that such experiences are a product of the human brain. It was the first experiment to ever prove that close encounters with UFOs and extraterrestrials are a product of the human mind. The experiment also demonstrated that alien contact is not indicative of the existence of otherworldly civilizations, but rather of a poorly studied state of consciousness that people occasionally fall into inadvertently."

Michael Raduga provides a fascinating free book download that details how to achieve out-of-body experiences; what he calls 'The Phase'. At the time of this writing, it is available for free download at http://obe4u.com/files/the_phase.pdf

Or you can contact him directly at obe4u@obe4u.com

Because of all the suggestions of 'it's only in your mind'; a person would need to provide some hard physical evidence of being abducted by aliens. This is one reason that so much attention was given to Betty Hill's 'star-map'. People were hopeful that it was a genuine artifact from an alien civilization. Let's look at a few more cases of Alien Abduction and then we will return to the subject of finding alien artifacts.

Chapter 4 - Alien Abduction Case 3

In December 1985, the writer Whitley Strieber experienced a terrifying alien abduction from his cabin in Upstate, New York. He wrote about his experience in a bestselling book, "Communion", which was later turned into a major film.

Whitley Strieber: "I woke up aware of the fact that there was something terribly wrong and when I opened my eyes I saw these dreadful figures around me, little stalky figures, they were dark blue, and a tall willowy sort of a figure that had big black eyes and a rather snout like sort of narrow face. And I thought I was, of course, I was having a nightmare. I kept trying to wake up again and I couldn't because I was already awake. I was… had, among other things, a needle stuck into the side of my head, it made a flash behind my eyes. It was absolutely terrifying. Then I blacked out."

Dr. David Jacobs: "One of the things that abductees have described over the years are these sort of unusual staring procedures where an alien will come in, stare directly into their eyes at a distance of a few inches, or one inch or even touching forehead to forehead.

And what is happening there is that the alien is sort of hooking into their optic nerve and using their optic nerve as a neural pathway. And by doing that, they can go all through their brain, stimulating or enervating any neural pathways that they want. And therefore, they can receive data, that is, you might say, they can look at an abductees' memories or what an abductee has been doing for the past few weeks or whatever. They can inject data if they wish, they can illicit emotional responses for whatever procedures they want to do, they can virtually control the person in any way they want."

Just what occurred up at the cabin remains a mystery. Strieber maintains that it was a real event and not a dream. And cites that over the following four years nineteen other people also reported seeing aliens at the same location.

Dr. Susan Blackmore gives a contrary opinion: "Alien abduction experiences could be one form of what's called a 'metachoric' experience. This is a particular kind of auto state of consciousness in which you think you're in the ordinary world, but in fact you've hallucinated everything. The most common example of this is the false awakening. There's where you dream that you've woken up. So, you're dreaming, you're dreaming you wake up, you perhaps get out of bed, clean your teeth, wander around, you know, everything's perfectly normal and then you see something isn't normal at all. 'Oh my god, I am dreaming!' and then you really wake up."

Interviewer: What's it like recounting the experience now after all these years?

Whitley Strieber: "It feels like it's happening again. It's as vivid as it was the day it happened. I'll never forget it for a second. It's burned into my brain. I remember it very well."

Nick Pope (Ministry of Defense): "I've met Whitley Strieber on a number of occasions and I am totally convinced that he's been entirely truthful about his experiences. He's undoubtedly someone who has undergone some quite extraordinary experience. Whether it's extraterrestrial or not, I don't know. I'm not sure that he would necessarily label it in that way. But it's alien certainly in the sense that it's alien to our understanding and I think that Whitley and people like him have clearly experienced something quite extraordinary."

The support group shown in the film "Communion" was based on a real abduction support group run by Budd Hopkins in New York City, which has met every week for the last 35 years.

Budd Hopkins (Abduction Counselor): "One of the things that's always asked by the abductees themselves: 'Why me?' Everybody's 'Why me?' And there's no answer for that. We have no idea. The one thing we do know is that if someone has been having abduction experiences, which they will have throughout their life again and again as if they're an involuntary specimen in somebody's long term study. And that person then comes to maturity and produces children of his or her own. It's very likely that one or more of those children will also be abducted. It's as if the aliens are following a particular genetic line."

Every Friday evening, around ten people come together in Hopkins' midtown house to share their experiences. For many it's a vital support mechanism in coping with the trauma.

Peter Robbins (Abduction Researcher): "What I feel is going on at the heart of the abduction phenomenon is that, another intelligence, from here or from another place is forcibly interacting with human beings. I feel it is against their will in a series of a priori, originally, perhaps experiments. And now a series of procedures that suggest a very disturbing situation, namely, that we're being mucked about with."

Chapter 5 - Alien Abduction Case 4

One of the most dramatic abduction cases that Hopkins investigated occurred in November 1989 in New York City to a woman name **Linda Napolitano**; she originally preferred to remain anonymous and used the alias **Linda Cortile**.

Linda: "Well, on November 30, 1989, I went to sleep and I felt this numbness crawling up from my toes up to my legs, and I felt a presence in the room. And I was afraid to open my eyes, and I didn't for a while, but then I had to in order to protect my family and myself, and when I opened my eyes there was this creature, this thing standing at the foot of my bed. It had large black eyes, it was sort of gray and it didn't belong there. I was terrified. I thought I was I was gonna have a heart attack to be quite honest with you. I thought I would go into heart failure. That's exactly how I felt."

Linda was put in touch with Budd Hopkins who undertook a series of hypnotic regressions. These sessions unlocked many more bizarre details of the abduction.

Linda: "Well, I found myself outside the window, 12 stories up in midair and I couldn't breathe. It was hard to breathe. And I felt as though my eyes were like stuck in their sockets, they wouldn't move, so all I could do was look straight ahead. I was bathed a bluish white light, sort of smoky and that was all I saw. And then the next thing I remembered was I felt as though I was on an invisible elevator going up and into this craft. Then I was brought into this very clinical looking room where I was undressed and I sat on this table. And they might have been about four creatures there. And they began to examine me."

Budd Hopkins: "One of the things about this subject is, if you see something dramatic or encountered somewhere through reading or whatever, one of the things is that you instantly realize is that, if this is true, it's the biggest event in human history. If there is in fact some non-human intelligence that is using some kind of non-human technology, suddenly interacting with us, it's the biggest event in human history. I can't imagine encountering this and not feeling dramatically moved and disposed to look into it."

According to those who investigated this abduction there were multiple witnesses who actually saw a UFO hovering over where the event occurred.

Yvonne Smith (Abduction Researcher): There were people that saw the craft hovering over her apartment building. When Budd shows the drawings from the different witnesses it's astounding and that's what we need to bring across to the public, is that these people aren't just abducted all by themselves in the middle of a field somewhere. This can happen anywhere."

Budd Hopkins (Abduction Counselor): "I have looked into probably about 620 separate individuals. And I've done numerous sessions with some of those people... So in a number of those cases I worked through maybe five, or six, or seven, or eight, ten abduction experiences. I've heard from another perhaps 4000 people by letter, telephone, face to face, descriptions that they were giving me but I didn't have the chance to follow them up. But the numbers are extraordinary."

Dr. David Jacobs: "What people say is that they're taken up out of their room, whether they are on their couch or kitchen, or wherever they are and often times they are floated directly through a closed window. And I've asked them 'Are you sure about this, that it was closed, didn't you open it or didn't they open it or did it open by themselves and the abductees are clear 'No, it's absolutely closed.' Now, if this was psychological, they will say 'Of course it was open'. There would be no problem then. But they look up at me and they say 'Has anybody else ever reported that? Floating through a closed window?' Not knowing that absolutely everybody reports that."

Interviewer: What would you think if it hadn't happened to you? In this neighborhood, with the people you know, if you'd been told that it happened to someone else. What would you have thought? What would your reaction be?

Linda: "I'd probably would not have believed it. I'd be very skeptical. And I expect most people to feel that way about my case. But I know what happened to me."

One of the major issues that skeptics have with the validity of Linda's abduction experience and the whole phenomenon in general was the use of hypnosis to unlock her memory of the event. Critics argue that this allows for the manipulation of the victim and in some cases the actual creation of a whole abduction experience.

Dr. Susan Blackmore (Psychologist) remains skeptical: "Imagine someone has had a deeply traumatic sleep paralysis experience. Imagine they woke up in the night, couldn't move, couldn't scream, felt creepy crawly fingers on them, had an awful sense that there's somebody in the room, heard buzzing and humming noises and then later on they woke up and it's all gone. What are they gonna think?

Now imagine that they go to a hypnotherapist, who regresses them and says 'You can remember, you can remember, you're lying on bed, the buzzing noises are there, you can remember.' Now, we know that hypnosis encourages fantasy, and they will fantasize. And they will probably fantasize about aliens, particularly if that particular hypnotherapist is known for doing alien abduction regressions. And so this fantasy, they'll know at the time it's a fantasy because you normally do in hypnosis. But it gradually works its way into their memory. And you've only got to do that a few times before your memory has become vivid and rich and absolutely convincing and you are sure that you were abducted. And in fact, you weren't."

Budd Hopkins: "Hypnosis, of course, has been the whipping boy of the skeptics because it's used very frequently in this. Hypnosis can very, very easily be misused. If a very clever interrogator can lead somebody in normal conversation, which we know is very possible, if you watch lawyers in action for instance, but even in just a normal conversation people can be lead, seduced, changed, almost against their will, so that the whole story becomes different. Under hypnosis it's even easier to do that."

Chapter 6 - Alien Abduction Case 5

Now we come to a case that is not as well known to the general public; a movie was never made about it; the participants did not seek any fame or fortune from their experience and yet it stands as one of the most startling cases of Alien Abduction ever recorded.

This incident occurred on the banks of the Pascagoula River on October 11th, 1973. Charles Hickson and Calvin Parker were planning on an evening of fishing but landed something beyond their wildest expectations. This interview was conducted in 1987:

Charles Hickson and Calvin Parker

Charles Hickson: "I don't think I'll ever forget what did happen, of course it was on October 11th of '73. I was employed by FB Walter & Son Shipyard at that time, Calvin was also, a friend of mine. Many evenings after work, I'd go fishing on the river when I'd have time so that day in particular at noon, Calvin and myself had planned on going fishing that evening after work.

After we, we had gone home and got our tackle of course, we went down to the river; we tried several places and we came back up to the old shipyard and I don't know whether…,what really attracted my attention but I heard a hissing like sound and when I turned and looked behind me there was something, some kind of craft. It was probably eighteen inches or a foot off the ground just hovering there. And there were two blue lights towards the front of it and they were either revolving or pulsing. And I really didn't know what to think; I didn't know what it was, it startled me at first. I stepped down off of the pier and looked around, I saw

Calvin stepped down too, he was doing the same thing I was; and about the time we stepped on the ground, there was a door opened there in the front, it just seemed to appear there, probably a sliding door.

There was a brilliant light that came out, from outside of the craft, just a beam of light. And there was something that, well I know now it was robots[7], but there was something that came into the door, there was three of them in fact, one behind the other one and they just seemed to glide out of the door; and they never touched the ground. I didn't know what to do, I'm quite frightened at that time; and the river's behind us, we couldn't go that way, so, and those things was getting close to us.

When they got up real close to me I guess I just froze, I don't know, then they came around and one of them took hold of this arm and I felt pain in it just

---

[7] A quote from Hickson: "After thinking more about it, I believe they were more like robots. They acted like they had a specific thing to do and they did it."

instantly and one of them took hold of the other arm. I seemed to just rise up from the ground at the height they were in more or less a leaning position.

They weren't very tall, I mean I'm five foot eight and I was a little taller than they were. And about that time, Calvin, he was to my right. I saw one take hold of him and he just went limp. And I found out later that he had passed out, he fainted from the fear I suppose. Anyway these things, we just went right on in to the craft through that door and that bright light; went in to probably was the middle of a room or compartment; it appeared to me it was round and the light was glowing from the walls and overhead and the floor.

We stopped about mid-ways in the room I suppose and they just released me. I couldn't move anything but my eyes, I could move my eyes, don't know why I could move them but not anything else. But anyway they released me and a few moments I suppose it was, but out directly in front of me something came out of the wall that appeared to me just a big, I always referred to it as an eye, a big pupil and eye. And it moved up in front of my face and remained there for a few moments, minutes I suppose and it went down and went under me and I'm assuming it went up the backside cuz it came back up over my head, came back in front of me and it remained there for a few more, probably a minute or two or more. And it moved back into the light in the wall and disappeared."

I was still suspended there, I didn't know, there wasn't anything I could do, I just kept wondering what are they gonna do with me? Are they gonna take me away or; I couldn't imagine what they were gonna do or what they were doing with me. But anyhow after a while these things came back and they took hold of me and we seemed to turn in the room and we moved back out of the doorway and they moved back almost to the exact spot that they had picked me up from and they just released me and I fell to the ground.

Well it was thing time that I saw Calvin again and he was, he was standing there in front of the river with his arms outstretched and he appeared to me to be going in shock. I was trying to get up on my feet to make it to him to see if I could help him some way and I heard that hissing sound again and I looked behind me and I saw those blue lights just instantly and this craft it just went away.

Well I made my way on to Calvin and I could get up on my feet by this time and it took me a while to get him where I could talk to him and assure him that maybe, you know, we weren't hurt bad I know but we really didn't know what they had done to us.

At first we decided we wouldn't tell anyone, we'd just keep it to ourselves because, you know, I didn't want to be called a nut and crazy; those things are just not supposed to happen. But the more I thought about it, the more I realized that we had to tell someone maybe the military because, you know possibly our country could be a threat to our country.

So we stopped on the way home, I called Keesler Air Force Base from a pay phone and briefly I tried to explain to them what had happened but they informed me that they didn't handle those things, that we'd have to go through the local sheriff's department.

Well we hesitated there, we didn't want to go through the sheriff's department because, you know, they might just grab us up and take us on to the nut house. But anyway we talked it over again and decided we would call the sheriff's department and maybe we could get them to assure us that we wouldn't have any publicity about it.

So I called the sheriff's department and they sent two deputies over which after talking with us asked us to follow them to the sheriff's department and we did. And they questioned us there for several hours and the sheriff assured me that night that we wouldn't have any publicity about it at all, he would maybe try to report it to the proper authorities; whoever the proper authorities were it could be investigated.

But the next day when we reached work my telephone was ringing and it was some reporter from

Jackson and then all the telephones at the shipyard started ringing. They were trying to get information about what happened to Charlie Hickson and Calvin Parker that past night in Pascagoula.

As a whole, I think the public has been real decent to me. I haven't had any ridicule over all these years; I think that's because I've been honest and when people wanted to ask me questions about it, I took up my time to do it.

Sometimes I think maybe I shouldn't have told anyone what happened to me on the Pascagoula river many years ago, but then again I realize that I did right by telling what happened. I think most of the people knows where man has been. I think I know where we are going; maybe someday I can help convince the world of that fact. I know there's other worlds out there with life on it and someday everyone will know that to be a fact without any doubt

In later life, Charles Hickson made these comments:

"There has to be a world out there somewhere, I don't know where it is, there has to be a world out there somewhere they come from.

***

Although not as well known as the Betty and Barney Hill case or the Travis Walton Case, this incident was also attacked by Philip Klass. Both men passed a polygraph but Philip Klass claimed the examiner was inexperienced. Others have brought up concerns that Calvin Parker changed his story in later years; that he eventually claimed he had not really passed out but had strange experiences on board the craft.

Charles Hickson passed away in 2011 at the age of 80. He never changed his story. In spite of detractors and the negative comments from skeptics, the Pascagoula Incident is one of the most compelling cases I have found in the area of Alien Abduction.

The day of the incident Hickson and Parker were interviewed by the local Sheriff and they played a kind of sneaky trick on the two men. They leave them alone by themselves at the police station in a room that had a hidden tape recorder. They figured that they would quickly know if they were cooking up a hoax by listening in on their private comments. The recording revealed that the men were in a genuine state of distress and shock at what they had just excperienced. Here is a partial transcript from that secret recording:

Calvin Parker: I almost had a heart attack and I ain't shitting you, I came one damn inch from dying.

Charlie Hickson: I know it scared me to death too. Jesus...have mercy.

Calvin Parker: I was standing there crying like, I just couldn't help it. What's so bad, nobody will believe us.

Charlie Hickson: I know it, I couldn't take much more of that. I thought I'd been through enough hell on this Earth, now I had to go through this.

Calvin: I tell you I need to get some pills or go see a doctor or something, I can't stand it, I'm about to go all crazy.

CHARLIE: I tell you, when we're through, I'll get you something to settle you down so you can get some damn sleep.

CALVIN: I can't sleep yet like it is. I'm just damn near crazy.

CHARLIE: Well, Calvin, when they brought you out- when they brought me out of that thing, goddamn it I like to never in hell got you straightened out.

CALVIN: My damn arms, my arms, I remember they just froze up and I couldn't move. Just like I stepped on a damn rattlesnake.

CHARLIE: They didn't do me that way.

CALVIN: I passed out. I expect I never passed out in my whole life.

CHARLIE: I've never seen nothing like that before in my life. You can't make people believe.

CALVIN: I don't want to keep sitting here. I want to see a doctor.
CHARLIE: They better wake up and start believing... they better start believing.

CALVIN: You see how that damn door come right up?

CHARLIE: I don't know how it opened, son. I don't know.

CALVIN: It just laid up and just like that those son' bitches-just like that they come out.

CHARLIE: I know. You can't believe it. You can't make people believe it-

CALVIN: I paralyzed right then. I couldn't move.

CHARLIE: They won't believe it. They gonna believe it one of these days. Might be too late. I knew all along they was people from other worlds up there. I knew all along. I never thought it would happen to me.

CALVIN: You know yourself I don't drink

CHARLIE: I know that, son. When I get to the house I'm gonna get me another drink, make me sleep. Look, what we sitting around for. I gotta go tell Blanche... what we waiting for?

CALVIN: I gotta go to the house. I'm getting sick. I gotta get out of here.

CALVIN: It's hard to believe . . . Oh God, it's awful... I know there's a God up there.

The day after the incident, Hickson and Parker were interviewed by the military at Keesler Air Force Base at which time it was revealed that others had also witnessed a UFO at the same corroborating their story including a Parole Officer by the name of Raymond Broadus.

A MUFO journal from 1984 published a report on the military interview that is included in Appendix 3. The military did not want to release this transcript and it interesting to see how it corroborates their testimony with the eyewintness accounts from a local parole office and a gas station attendant.

Charlie Hickson always said he thought he remained conscious throughout the experience but he also admitted that he might have lost consciousness since he didn't exactly remember leaving the craft; it was more like he just found himself back outside again.

The Pascagoula Incident remains as one the more compelling cases of Alien Abduction to this day.

Chapter 7 - More Problems with Memories

Dr. Susan Blackmore: "Now, what we know about the way normal memory works, is the more often you tell a story the more you are inclined to remember the story you told rather the original event. And at its most extreme this can become what's called false memory, where a memory can feel absolutely real like a memory and yet has been created by your own telling of the story."

So, are abductees really experiencing what they say or are they making it all up? Leah Haley claims she was abducted several times from her home in Gulf Breeze, Florida, and then taken into what she describes as an alien spacecraft. She wrote several books on the subject and now lectures on alien abductions around the world. Although her memories of the event were solely recovered under hypnosis, she maintains they really did happen to her.

Leah Haley: "I didn't remember everything about the experience, but I did remember being in a round room that had a very bright, intense light, and I was lying on a flat platform on my back and I remembered aliens standing all around me performing medical experiments on me. They had solid black eyes, two little holes for nose. I couldn't remember a mouth at all, they didn't have any hair, they didn't have any ears. And I remember that I felt very calm, not afraid at all. But it was like I was paralyzed. I couldn't just get up and move around. I was like a medical subject."

Like many abductees, Leah suffered alienation and derision from her friends and family after she went public. Despite this, she stands by her story and now campaigns for this phenomenon to be taken seriously.

Leah Haley: "I got fired from a job that I loved because I felt that it was important to go public with my story. My older daughter who was 24 years old disowned me because I went public with my story. She got married last July. I was not invited to the wedding. I was told by my own child that she never wanted to hear from me again. She never wanted to see me again. As far as she was concerned, I was dead because I had embarrassed the family by talking about my experiences."

Keen to prove that she was telling the truth, she agreed to allow a former FBI profiler, Paul Minor, to carry out a detailed polygraph examination on her.

Paul Minor: "I was a polygraph examiner for the army up until 1978. And at that time I went over to the FBI and I was the chief polygraph examiner for the FBI from 1978 till the end of 1987, when I left and set up my own business, a security firm in Fairfax, Virginia.

Paul Minor: Do you intend to lie to me in any way during this polygraph test?"

Leah Haley: "No.

Paul Minor: "Do you claim to have been abducted by alien beings?"

Leah Haley: "Yes!

Paul Minor: "Are you lying about being gynecologically examined by aliens in a spacecraft?"

Leah Haley: "No.

Paul Minor: "Are you afraid that you might pass this polygraph test?"

Leah Haley: "Yes!

Leah Haley:

"It seemed very real, just as real as my being here conscious, talking right now. It was very difficult for me to accept the reality of it. I tried to explain it away as a dream. I said to myself: 'How could aliens get into my house? All the doors and windows were locked. But it seemed so real that I had to go and check every door and window and convince myself that they were all locked.

The polygraph exam is extremely nerve wracking and stressful to take the exam because one doesn't know how accurately a machine reads the material. It's like, I know I'm telling the truth, but how can a machine tell if I'm telling the truth or not?"

Interviewer: Tell me how she now did on the test, that she passed or failed.

Paul Minor: "It showed that she was deceptive and not only is it my opinion, but she was strongly deceptive, but there's a program in the computer here that was done by John Hopkins University and I scored the charts on that and it says deception strongly indicated, the probability of deception being greater than .99. So, that's almost certain.

Interviewer: So there were no doubts in your mind that she was trying to deceive us?

Paul Minor: "No doubt in my mind."

Interviewer: There's not even an element that she believes it, that it may not have happened to her?

Paul Minor: "No, if she believed it would show that she was telling the truth. But it showed that she does not believe it and she knows that this did not occur."

Professor Chris French (Psychologist, University of London): "Certainly, in some cases where individuals have reported full blown abduction experiences, independent witnesses who were present in the room with them at the time reported that physically they had not left the room. In other words, the entire experience was taking place inside their own heads. Now, if we know that that can happen in some cases, I think the burden of proof is then on those who are making the stronger claims that people really are being taken aboard flying sources to show that that's not what's happening in all of the cases."

Another problem with memories is that it is impossible to determine if a person's memories may have been altered by the event itself or by direct alien manipulation. For example here is a case that was only documented publicly on October 16th, 2013 but the original event occurred in 1964. In his account Mike Hyde gives details which indicate a specific case of inconsistent memories from the original eyewitnesses:

Mike Hyde UFO Report:

"This is an incident I witnessed as a 6 year old boy. We lived at 2008 N. Sherman Blvd. Grand Island, NE. The neighborhood was fairly new at the time and compared to today, was on the fringes of several farms and quasi-rural. The northern major road running east/west was Capitol Ave. and one block south was State St. Young kids in the neighborhood attended West Lawn Elementary (not the new one, but rather the old one at State St. & Broadwell).

This above image is the view looking to the north on N. Sherman which was right in front of our house. There were not many trees back then as the neighborhood was very new. There were even fewer houses. Most of the houses feature here on the right were not built until 1965/1966. So the view northward was very open and clear all the way up to Capitol.

On Saturday, August 8th, 1964 a lot of the neighborhood kids and I were out playing in the street. It was typical stuff; riding bikes, playing Army, simply running all over the place. A lot of parents were out working on their yards, washing their cars, etc. Just a typical hot and very humid day in Central Nebraska.

An object drifted over the sky, transiting NW to SE on its flight path. It got everyone's attention pretty quick. It was huge. Far bigger than a modern airship or similar type of craft. It was slightly overcast that day, but you could see it clearly. It was black, shaped like an oval cylinder. It had a red line going around the middle of it that was lit up and appeared almost electrical in nature. I remember smelling ozone. Like you do when you short a wire out or with lightning. At the bottom and slightly to the side was some type of opening or even possibly a light source that was intense blue-white. It was not a beam or anything, at least it did not appear that way. It makes me think it was an opening as it appeared and then disappeared a couple of times. I do not recall anything coming out of it. But there was a strange sound, almost like ringing in your ears – but it was a really high frequency. It didn't hurt or anything, but it was there.

People were talking about it and my Dad (who cannot remember it happening) said it was probably some kind of USAF aircraft. One of the neighbors, my friend David Phelps' grandfather thought it was probably something the Russians had cooked up to scare people with. The odd thing in this was the longer it hovered there, the more quiet everyone got and soon stopped talking altogether. They just stared at it. Even my friend David and another friend, a girl named Polly stopped talking and just stared at it. No one spoke, no one moved. I think at some point that the same happened to me.

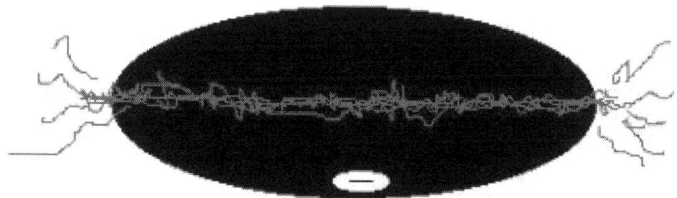

This is approximately what the object looked like. I am guessing here, but I believe it may have been as large as a ¼ mile in length. It was simply massive.

I have no recollection of time between the incident and Sunday dinner, which was the next day. I do not know what happened in that time period, as the next day we were getting in my Dad's Valiant and heading over to my grandmother's house on 4th Street.

Most of the kids there that day are haunted by this incident. They know it happened, but none of the adults remember anything at all. **It is like their memories were erased.** This has haunted me for 50 years. I remember it as clear as daylight."

***

This remarkable incident is significant in that it describes vividly a situation in which memories are strangely altered. Everyone has seen the 'Men-in-Black' comedies where a silly device is used to erase memories but all parodies aside; this is a very common phenomenon that seems to occur when close alien contact occurs that must be kept in mind when considering the topic of alien abduction or any alien encounter for that matter.

Chapter 8 - Messages Delivered

In Northern Wisconsin in 1975, Karen Klinger and Dennis Muraskwa were on a family vacation when they decided to go for a walk together. They noticed something in the night sky.

Karen Klinger: "We saw bright orange star that was along the horizon of the trees on the other side of the lake and then it zipped near the top of our heads."

Dennis Muraska: "I thought you could describe the flight as that of a dragonfly. It would just zip her and stop and then zip here and stop; zip, zip, zip really fast and I was like 'what are we watching?' I finally started to call my folks down from the cabin so they could watch and my mother was a little scared."

Karen Klinger: "Dennis sister's boyfriend went into the house and grabbed a large beam flashlight and used it to flash at the UFO three times. Suddenly they just completely disappeared. And then about, maybe a couple of seconds later, they flashed back at us the same amount of times we had flashed at it."

Dennis Muraska: "By this time we knew we were watching something that we had no explanation for; it was really strange and definitely seemed to be intelligently controlled."

After the incident, Muraska and Klinger felt disoriented and ill. Later when the couple talked about the incident, they realized they could not account for several hours during that night.

Dennis Muraska: "At one point we looked up and the moon was directly in line with the rear view mirror of the car and by the time we got back to the lake which shouldn't have been very long, the moon was setting."

Karen Klinger: "It never occurred to me until that moment, that there could possibly be some missing time involved. When I realized that, I felt sick, I literally felt nauseated at the thought of it."

In search of more answers, Dennis and Karen each underwent hypnosis.

Dennis Muraska: "We compared notes later and they corroborated very closely with some of the points that Karen brought up under hers. We bought got these images of a grid-like pattern."

The apparent purpose of their abduction was to make those touched to become the carrier of a message that is: 'The Earth is connected to the universe.'

Karen Klinger: "If you feel that this has happened to you, by all means do whatever it takes to uncover the information, because it's worth the risk."

***

Another individual who claims to have received messages via abduction is Steve Neill. He tells people that aliens have alerted him to the fact that the human race needs help.

Steve Neill: "We've separated ourselves from nature, we have the sense that nature's over there and we're over here and that nature was kind of made for us to do whatever we want; to trash it in the name of personal gain or profit. I think that we're in danger of becoming extinct like the dinosaurs."

On many of his abductions Neill has been shown horrific images of the future.

"They take me into the scene, whether it's you know the world after a nuclear war; they take me right down the streets and I see all the bodies and the whole bit. I realize that they're trying to give me a message you know and I'm supposed to take this message of this possible future and do something about it and try to present it."

For other abductees similar terrifying visions have led them to form or join a support group. Most of them feel that the images or messages they receive from aliens are a warning and that humans have the power to alter their destiny.

Chapter 9 - Alien Artifacts

It would seem that if a person who was abducted came back with something physical from his alien encounter, it would be proof positive that his or her abduction experience was genuine. There is a doctor who believes that he has obtained such evidence; his name is Dr. Roger Leir. Here are some documented details about his work:

Dr. Roger Leir is a surgeon from Southern California who has been performing operations on patients for over thirty years.

Dr. Roger Leir: "So far, eight surgeries have been performed and with the eight surgeries we have removed nine objects. The commonality of course is that all the individuals are subjects of the alien abduction phenomenon."

In 1996 he performed one of the first surgeries to remove an alien implant from the jaw of an alleged abductee.

Dr. Roger Leir: "The gentleman that we did the surgery on, for the procedure to remove an object from the left jaw was in private industry and he had a history of alien abduction."

As with most abductees, the patient was reluctant to come forward or to have his face publicly shown.

Dr. Roger Leir: "There is a certain stigma involved with abductees; they have innate fear about telling somebody about what happened. They may feel that they may lose their job or their career may be in jeopardy, even financial loss so there's some very practical things involved.

Dr. Leir describes some of the extraordinary findings discovered during this amazing surgery: "There is no portal of entry; there is no evidence how the object got inside the body. Then when we looked at tissue surrounding the object we found there was no inflammatory response; this is impossible because anything that enters the body should have an inflammatory response. And then thirdly they are surrounded by a large number of nerve proprioceptors which are not anatomically correct.

Once the outer biological membrane was removed, it revealed a triangular shaped object, this object was housed in yet another grey membrane; remarkably this inner membrane could not be cut even with a surgical scalpel.

Close up image of alien implant

The implant was then sent to Los Alamos National Laboratory for metallurgic testing.

Dr. Leir: "We knew that when we got the initial report back from Los Alamos that we didn't have something that was common because Los Alamos is a world class laboratory and would not recommend further testing on anything that they didn't feel was strange. So it was the combination of elements that were in these objects that I think inspired them to advise us that more tests be done."

The implant was then sent to New Mexico Tech Laboratory where a battery of metallurgic tests were performed on the object.

Dr. Leir: The theory that they put forth was that these were portions of meteorites. They did not know that they were removed from a human body.

Amazingly the New Mexico Tech lab report revealed that the elements in the implant were composed of meteorites so rare, only a few had ever been found. At this point, scanning electron microscope analysis was conducted on the implant. The result revealed the implants were manufactured and not naturally occurring meteorites. Results showed the implants had been connected to the patients nerve endings.

Dr. Leir: "The second set of tests following some of tests at New Mexico was run by University of California at San Diego."

The laboratory results from UCSD confirmed the earlier tests, a portion of the metal analyzed in the implant was extraterrestrial and did not come from Earth.

Dr. Leir: "Some of the elements that were found, in combinations, were of non-terrestrial origin, extra-terrestrial origins.

The evidence is overwhelming and the implications are staggering. In each case, the chain of evidence has been documented and the test results are shocking.

Dr. Leir: This could be the proof that science has been looking for. The implications of this discovery are worldwide and affect every single living human being.

***

Of course Dr. Leir is not without his detractors. Penn & Teller did a skeptical blurb on his work in one of their HBO videos and there are many brief articles that question his work. If Dr. Leir could get additional corroboration from other medical professionals or if he could get one of his patients to come forward publicly with their story of the circumstances surrounding how they were implanted, this would add a lot of weight to the evidence he is presenting.

Chapter 10 - A Worldwide Phenomenon

Although the vast majority of abductions reports come from the United States, it is in fact a worldwide phenomenon, with thousands of cases being reported in the United Kingdom alone. The man who was responsible for investigating these reports, on behalf of the UK government was Nick Pope.

Nick Pope: "Whilst it's true to say that other people within various governments have conducted official research into UFOs, which has mirrored the work that I did at the ministry; to the best of my knowledge, I am the only person in the world ever to have conducted *official* research and investigation into the alien abduction phenomenon.

Some people said to me when I was at the ministry 'Why are you wasting time looking into alien abductions?' I said, as long as people report these experiences to me, I have a duty to take their claims seriously. Some of these people were phoning up in a great state of distress. What was I supposed to do? Hang up on them?"

One of his cases was Peter and Diane Shepard, who saw a large, brightly lit UFO outside their house in the country.

Diane Shepard: "There, in front of us, across the road, the main road, were the most amazing lights in the sky to our left. There were quite a number of them and they were actually coming from our left, crossing over the road, and then they were coming in front of us and going to the right."

Peter Shepard: "This was a field length away by the way. These lights were tree-top height, but around the red was like a high low effect of flashing, sparkling, brilliant white flashes were going off."

Diane Shepard: "We were all stunned at what we were seeing. Our reality was completely shattered. This was something that wasn't supposed to happen,"

Peter Shepard: "How can something... you know... how could this be? This is a shattering experience. You can't believe it. I was excited, a little bit frightened, a little bit uneasy because of the size of this thing. It was awesome."

Prof. Chris French: "The basic experience itself, I wouldn't dispute. Often it did seem to that person to take place the way they describe it. The question is how we interpret what happened. Did they just have some kind of very rich and complex hallucination and that's what was happening?"

Another bizarre case was Ann and Paul Andrews, whose son, Jason, was repeatedly visited by a UFO throughout his childhood. On each occasion, their house would begin to shake wildly, a bright light would come through the doors and windows and Jason would make his way to the front door and out into their garden. He would disappear for hours on end.

Ann Andrews: "I mean, the initial reaction is absolute terror. You know, you're running around like a headless chicken. You don't know if you have to phone the police or what to do. You're just sort of standing there, that you know, just screaming at each other. The second reaction is anger, you know real anger that this can happen. Why can you not do anything about it? It's like when Jason was younger. He would come to us and say 'I hate them for taking me, but I hate you for not stopping them.' You feel very angry. You feel very frustrated. And you also feel very upset that this is going on sort of in your own home, in your own house where you are supposed to protect your children and keep them safe and you can't do anything about it."

Nick Pope: "Some people have speculated that what we are dealing with, when we talk about the grays; is with what humans one day evolve into. And it's been suggested that we are dealing with people from the future coming back through time to take genetic material, perhaps to revitalize the human race."

Ann Andrews: "He told us that was what was happening to him. I mean, he told us for years that he was being taken away by little men. I mean, this was when he was four or five. He said 'These little men come into my room and they make me go away with them'. Of course, we said nobody can get in, the doors are locked, mommy and daddy are here to protect you, all the things that parents say. So it was him that was insisting to us that this is what was going on."

Paul Andrews: "I'd like to know why. And if I could, I'd stop it."

Nick Pope (investigator at UK Ministry of Defense): "At the end of the day, **my best assessment and because this is a view I formed at the ministry, I guess you could call an official assessment, is that yes,**

we are dealing with extraterrestrials and yes, the alien abduction phenomenon is real in a physical sense."

So what is going on? Are thousands of people really being abducted against their will by aliens? Are sinister experiments being carried out on the human race in spacecrafts?

Perhaps the most unique take on the phenomenon is from the British scientist Albert Budden. He spent years researching the idea that alien abductions aren't real physical events but are severe mental reactions caused by exposure to high levels of electromagnetic energy. Interestingly, only a very small percentage of people are sensitive enough to be affected by this phenomenon which causes the victim to produce vivid and entirely life like hallucinations.

Albert Budden: "All these abductees or experiences are actually suffering from a developed condition called electrical hypersensitivity. And this long word means that they are hypersensitive to the invisible electromagnetic energies in the environment and they are living in something called a hotspot, where the electromagnetic energies are higher than most places. There are near power lines, near radio transmitters, over a crack in the earth which is a geological fault which produces electromagnetic fields. Near a transformer; there is a whole host of sources of electromagnetism in the environment – a local source, there are many kinds of this, a radio ham next door, a CB radio enthusiast a few yards away. All of these things will radiate a house on a permanent basis."

According to Button's research, the sensations reported by abductees mirror those of people who are affected by strong electromagnetic currents.

"They have periods when they feel that there is somebody in the room with them, watching them although they can't actually see anybody; they call it a sense of presence. Their sense of time will be distorted, it's called a sense of de-synchronization, where they feel that time has gone by in a flash or that time has been distorted or drawn out, there is a whole host of signs and symptoms that they begin to suffer from after being exposed to high levels of electromagnetism."

Unfortunately Budden's theory cannot explain how two people (Like the case of Paul and Ann Andrews) could experience the same 'hallucination' – such an explanation in a case like that is clearly implausible.

So, are alien abductions real? Are people being beamed up into spaceships and subjected to bizarre experiments? Or is this just all some sort of severe psychological disorder? Abductees themselves have no doubt that it is a real phenomenon. And yet the hard physical evidence is very thin to almost non-existent.

At the end of the day this is a phenomenon that seems to affect millions of people around the world. And until we find out the true cause, the abduction files will remain firmly open.

Budd Hopkins: "The whole basic purpose seems to be that the UFO occupants have reached some kind of evolutionary dead end, that's an assumption but I think it's a fairly safe one. And that they need to revivify their own stock, so to speak with something, probably something more primitive than we can offer them, that they seem to need. This seems to be for them, not for us. We have no idea where this program is going to end up. But many people have described seeing on ships and, in experiences figures that seem to be a mix of human and alien characteristics."

Dr. Susan Blackmore: "In the end my own impression is that the vast majorities of alien abductions experiences are in fact in sleep paralysis. That people have woken up paralyzed as from dreaming. But they are half awake, they can't move, they have all the classic symptoms of sleep paralysis buzzing, humming, bright light, the feeling of presence of somebody there, and their mind takes over and does the rest, and clothes the whole thing in all the paraphernalia of an alien abduction."

Nick Pope: "The biggest problem with alien abduction research at the moment is that with the best will in the world it's been carried out by a handful of dedicated amateurs. What we really need to take forward research into this important matter is the involvement of mainstream science and the involvement of government. It's only these two bodies that really I think can take this forward and perhaps achieve some sort of breakthrough."

Leah Haley: "Abduction is horrifying, abduction is a nightmare, but the audience must know that these events are real; the physical events that have happened to millions of people; and I would not be surprised if someone you know is an abductee, but they have never said it."

Afterword

There is, without a doubt, a vast amount of documented alien abduction cases. By their very nature, the accounts are often confusing, scary and difficult to analyze objectively. There may come a time when the veil is pulled away and humankind is able to see clearly what is behind all these encounters. Perhaps the future will see a friendly and open relationship between an alien population and the human population. Imagine a world where intergalactic neighbors are able to work together in a relationship that brings benefits to all life forms.

But then again, perhaps the future holds as yet unknown dangers from alien visitors; either from malicious intent or unintentional contamination. There is no way of knowing for certain which of these scenarios is more likely; all we can do in the meantime is to keep alert to our circumstances and remain diligent in documenting all cases of alien activity as they occur.

May your future be one of hope, peace and increasing knowledge.

~ Sean Keyhoe

Appendix 1 – Betty Hill Interview from 1999 Continued

Interviewer: So Barney, I mean life going on as usual, you did mention this, not that you have the total memory blockages of what happened but you knew what happened but it wasn't dramatically affecting your lives, you were curious more than anything.

Betty Hill: Curiosity.

Interviewer: At that point now Walter Webb representing NICAP comes. Does he get involved in the picture?

Betty Hill: He interviewed us a couple of times.

Interviewer: Interviewed you, Walter's a very highly esteemed researcher, one of the original…

Betty Hill: Well you see, actually I would say three weeks after this happened, he got involved.

Interviewer: Did you notice anything strange, odd vehicles around your home, were you followed?

Betty Hill: No, no.

Interviewer: Your prototypical men in black, did you see any of those?

Betty Hill: No they called us from Washington. They heard about our experience, they would like to meet us, they were scientists, they had an interest in UFOs and so they came. We had continued contact for years, so the United States Government. One time we even got together and camped out we got twenty six of the top scientists.

Interviewer: Wow. So there was no subversion or subterfuge going on with the government, they were straightforward out of curiosity and no-one was mocking you or highly skeptical.

Betty Hill: Oh they were looking for information.

Interviewer: Because this was a highly unique case and it represented a different genre in the UFO phenomenon where it was a close encounter of the third kind? Or would you call it a fourth kind where you were abducted, I know that those are the classifications given by Dr. Hinack. It was a landed craft, you saw it then you went on board it.

Betty Hill: And the men who came, they were in touch with us from the White House, the National Security

Council, NASA and let's see...they were the top of government.

Interviewer: The big guys.

Betty Hill: Right. They said, we want to know the facts; we don't want you even with the possibility of being influenced by something else. And I still have contacts.

Interviewer: The spring of 1962, problems start happening with Barney; what's going on with Barney?

Betty Hill: Well, Barney started to; his blood pressure was fluctuating and he was having anxiety, you see Barney was working the midnight shift too so he's driving to Boston every night, had to be there at midnight and he's getting home at 7 or 8 o'clock in the morning. He's trying to sleep during the day and everything just built up and he got sick physically.

Interviewer: Lack of sleep can compound itself. At that point did you equate back to the incident of September 19th, did you think it was directly related? Was he having nightmares or he just couldn't get sleep?

Betty Hill: No. He couldn't sleep and he would; before we started going to doctors, he would leave here to go to Boston to go to work and turn around and come home and he was just like, "I can't do it". He was too exhausted. "I don't feel good."

Interviewer: And then doctor Simon.

Betty Hill: No, he was going to his regular family doctor who was prescribing medications trying to treat him and he's not improving. So his doctor thought maybe he had some kind of emotional problem that was preventing him from feeling so he sent him in to a psychiatrist in the same office building he was in. So Barney's gotta go in to Dr. Stevens on a regular basis, and he's talking about his childhood and his mother and his father, you know. And one day doctor Stevens said, "What did you do this weekend?" and Barney told him he went up in the White Mountains looking for UFOs. And then Barney told him and he's the one who referred us to Dr. Benjamin Simon who was one of his teachers in medical school.

Interviewer: Doctor Simon puts both of you under hypnosis, records...

Betty Hill: Now let me get it straight about hypnosis; what you hear and what you see is stage hypnosis, we had medical hypnosis which is the kind that's used in surgery.

Interviewer: Medical hypnosis, it's a highly trained psychologist or a doctor as opposed to a charlatan with a watch dangling back and forth.

Betty Hill: Right. And Doctor Simon at the end of World War Two had been the director of the Mason General Hospital in New York City for the treatment of servicemen coming back from World War Two who had emotional problems. And he was so highly successful using medical hypnosis that the U.S. Army did a documentary of Doctor Simon's work. And in the beginning it was two hours long. But then in 1980, around there somewhere, they shortened it to one hour and it was shown on Public PBS stations and the name of the film is 'Let There Be Light'. And it, if you could a hold of it, it is one of the greatest things you ever saw.

Interviewer: So this man has a lot of badges I guess; in the field of psychiatry. He's not somebody that would lead questions. Like you said, he brought a lot of men out of battle fatigue who were emotionally scarred in combat. And the casualties in World War One alone of shellshock, men if they have been treated by trained physicians could have been saved and brought back to normality.

Betty Hill: There was a serviceman brought in a wheelchair, he can not walk; he had been hit by shrapnel, it had all been removed, there was no reason in the world why he couldn't walk except he couldn't. So he's lying on the bed, Dr. Simon puts him in medical hypnosis and he says to him, "Get up and walk." He gets out of bed and walks. And he's walking around the room. Goes over to the nurse and he's crying saying, "Look, look , I can walk. I can really walk." Dr. Simon puts him back in to bed, brings him out of the hypnosis and the first thing he does, looks at Dr. Simon with a real worried look on his face and says, "Do you think I will ever be able to walk?" And Dr. Simon says, "I'm sure you will." At the end of the movie, it shows him out playing baseball.

Interviewer: So Dr. Simon could help people will their way through agony. This is brought to the public's attention in 1968 or then a movie was made. You were known through newspaper accounts but you known worldwide or maximum publicity was reached when the movie was made.

Betty Hill: In 1965, a reporter from a Boston newspaper heard about our experience and without ever meeting us published it for five days on the front pages of the newspaper. It went all over the world from that moment.

Interviewer: Without having met you, he took liberties with the story and there were some inaccuracies.

Betty Hill: He was pretty accurate. I still don't know who his source was.

Interviewer: Do you think maybe one of your government contacts had leaked this information to him and then orchestrated some how to get to the public consciousness?

Betty Hill: I never thought of that, I don't know.

Interviewer: What myths do you want to dispel about your encounter; things they fail to mention; if you can think of any. I've learned some stuff tonight; I always thought they were almond-shaped entities but you said they were very much human-like. They spoke to you verbally as opposed to telepathically.

Betty Hill: I had a great time; wait a minute, I'll go get junior so you can see what junior looks like. Another thing, I never called them aliens. Astronauts, I call them what they were. This is a composite, there was as much difference among them as there is among any group of people.

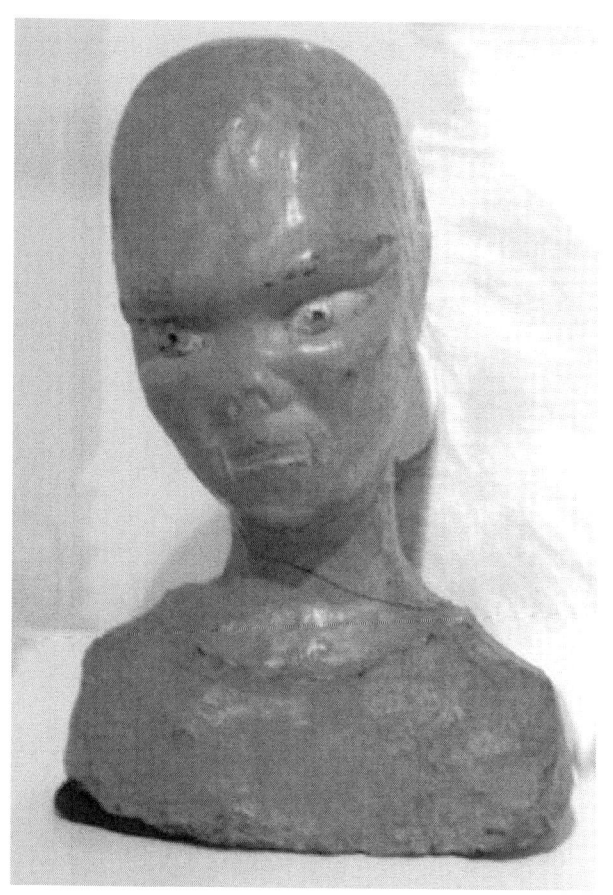

Betty Hill's 'Junior'

Betty Hill: This basically shows the characteristics, the larger eyes, the nose, the mouth, no protruding ears, no hair.

Interviewer: He has a pronounced brow ridge.

Betty Hill: Yup.

Interviewer: A pug nose, more or less a small orifice for a mouth and actually had yellow eyes.

Betty Hill: We put yellow in to emphasize them.

Interviewer: I was gonna say, he needs Visine or looks like he has Malaria but...

Betty Hill: Okay now, Junior has been evaluated by I don't know how many physical anthropologists but what he looks like now, if we continue on the path of evolution, this is what we're going to look like in 25,000 years.

Interviewer: And would we be mammalian, reptilian or insectoid or a combination of all three, I mean because if you look at the way we're on our way with the nuclear, there was a nuclear exposure in Japan for instance and radiation causes mutation and if you look along the lines of evolution, we lost our appendix for instance; people say we'll lose our little toe because we don't need it. The brain capacity gets larger, you become more spindly because you don't need muscles because it's mind over matter, correct?

Betty Hill. No.

Interviewer: Okay.

Betty Hill: It's gonna be like we are now except; I mean look mankind has been around what 2.6 million years?

Interviewer: Depends on who you talk to I guess. Subjective.

Betty Hill: Well, look at the bodies.

Interviewer: So that's basically what the astronaut looked like.

Betty Hill: Right.

Interviewer: Can I ask you something, when they put that needle, back on board the craft, when they put that needle intoyour navel, some have speculated that perhaps they were taking eggs or ova?

Betty Hill: No.

Interviewer: No, you don't think so. Because some have projected, isn't that interesting if you correlate that with test tube babies years ago...

Betty Hill: Well of course you know at the time this happened they it's absolutely impossible to put a needle in someone's navel, they would get an infection; and I think the process has been developed down in Houston, Texas.

Interviewer: Shortly afterward. Did they perform any function like that with Barney then?

Betty Hill: No.

Interviewer; None whatsoever.

Betty Hill: Nothing sexual whatsoever.

Interviewer: That's another myth dispelled. There was always an overtone, to get that clarified.

Betty Hill: Absolutely no sexual, in fact , they have these different methods of producing children, maybe we won't have any sex in 25,000 years.

Interviewer: Well maybe I won't go there but it's even tough in 1999 let me tell you.

Betty Hill: Laughs.

Interviewer: After this incident, you catapulted into the limelight; are people relaying similar experiences? You start hearing from people who have similar experiences and you are probably saying, these people are imagining on the one hand, others are very legitimate.

Betty Hill: First of all, as soon as our experience became known, we became a central point for people to report sightings. And then after the movie, 'The UFO Incident', then we had people; the movie was in '75 and that was after Barney's death; they were calling me saying, "Oh, I think I've been abducted." And so then as a social worker; and I used Doctor Simon's formula; when people tell a weird tale, it could be hallucinations, delusions, fantasies or they're recalling something they've seen, heard or read. When you rule out all those, then you may have the truth.

Interviewer: People tried to equate that you had taken from the Vilas-Boas case. Vilas-Boas was a Latin man who was abducted or claimed to be abducted by a spaceship and I guess was sexually accosted by a female alien on board a spaceship and skeptics like Phil Klass, if you wanna go after Phil right now, you can.

Betty Hill: He isn't that important, I would tell Phil he only acts that way because he tries to make money on my reputation.

Interviewer: Let's go there for the skeptic. I'm know as a para-skeptic. If you believe I probably don't, if you don't I probably do; I amalgamate my theories from both schools of thought; you're both right, you're both wrong. There are some on the far end of this alien culture that have these impossible stories that I cannot comprehend and then there are the absurd close-minded skeptics who will denounce anything without even giving the possibility that this instance could be real. I think that if there's; I come upon something that's unexplained, my job's complete. I'm looking for hoaxes and I'm looking for mis-identifications let someone else figure it out.

Betty Hill: Now let me say this, if I was abducted, there are real, honest-to-God abductions, but they're not known to the public. I know probably about twelve and most of them involve two or three people and fifty percent of those people who have been abducted are in the emergency room of a hospital within four to six hours.

Interviewer: Because they're convulsing or…

Betty Hill: No, no. They have breathing difficulties, they lose their sense of balance, their eyes won't focus, there are different…two men in Maine had brown and yellow marks around their necks, around their eyes, different parts of their bodies.

Interviewer: Was this the Allagash incident?

Betty Hill: No.

Interviewer: So they were traumatized, unknown to the public, very violent with physical traces left over, the physical repercussions.

Betty Hill: I mean there's something more than just saying, "Oh, I think I've been abducted." And they've called the police and said, 'take me to a hospital'.

Interviewer: You don't consider yourself an abductee but a passenger, a tour, I mean do you consider yourself an abductee?

Betty Hill: No.

Interviewer: Even though the popular literature points to you and Barney as the first abductees.

Betty Hill: No, we had a meeting, I mean like Columbus came here and the Indians.

Interviewer: A cosmic caucus. So the movie comes on, you're a clearing house for information, a lot of people come to you; some stories you can't believe, others you see are truly traumatized and victimized. They ask 'what can you do to help me', you probably answer, 'I can't do anything but you can only take consolation that others have shared your same experience'. Was that your advice to abductees? That's my advice to abductees.

Betty Hill: Well, if anybody comes to me and says I think I've been abducted, the first thing I say is "stay away from me", UFO investigators, "do not have hypnosis", and then if you've really been abducted, you'll begin to remember it yourself. You don't need anybody to tell you, and you will begin, and you will gradually remember the whole thing.

Such as John Salza who was teaching at the college in North Dakota and he got in touch with me. He said, "I think my son and I have been abducted; both of them were in colleges only his son was teaching in California, the father was teaching in North Dakota and the two of them would get together and go into Mississippi on this trip when it happened.

They come back home and they are separated and both of them begin to recall exactly what happened. No hypnosis, no nothing, they remembered the whole thing.

Interviewer: The UFO investigators start calling you but the government is calling you. Scientists from all branches, like you said, military intelligence, I'm sure Universities. Everybody has a solid scientific inquiry; there is no skepticism at that point because of your sincerity and your consistency of testimony.

Betty Hill: Well, for about five years I guess, I did college lectures which is a lot of fun.

Interviewer: Sure, I mean meeting the young people, the young minds.

Betty Hill: You see, I invited the UFO's to come down and they did; not here but a few miles from here. And we went out, we had volunteers, we covered the area almost every night for about fifteen years.

Interviewer: Okay.

Betty Hill: And we had scientists, we had labs, testing equipment, we had the military. Half the people that lived in town observed it. And we got loads and loads of information about UFOs but we also got hundreds and hundreds of pictures.

Interviewer: Sightings over a fifteen year period in southern New Hampshire, you orchestrated watch groups.

Betty Hill: Only volunteers and when I did the college lecture tours, I used about eighty-five different slides of UFOs but not just UFOs; UFO's doing different kinds of things. Like a carrier with nine gifts coming out of it.

Interviewer: Wow.

Betty Hill: I had an eight-nine dollar movie camera.

Interviewer: And you have a film of a mother-ship.

Betty Hill: Actually what I did is I sent them, movie film to a friend who is a psychiatrist, projected the movie film onto the screen and then took his camera and snapped slides. And then I showed the slides in my lectures. And I've got...people don't realize what a huge variety of different kinds and shapes of UFOs there are. And also they're usually travelling around in a squadron of between one hundred and fifty and two hundred. So if you see one UFO keep looking; there's an awful lot more – they don't travel alone, that's why the militay doesn't attack them.

Interviewer: How many different types of entities or races of people; for instance you met some from Zeta Reiculi, how many different, are they all from Zeta Reticuli?

Betty Hill: I have no idea, all I know is these craft are flyingtogether in squadrons.

Interviewer: Okay. Emanating from the same solar system.

Betty Hill: I don't know where they are coming from.

Interviewer: Okay, and they travel in squadrons, and this is only based on visual observations that you've taken personally. For instance, how many UFO's have you see do you think? It's impossible hundreds we'll just say right?

Betty Hill: Thousands.

Interviewer: You can't see them on demand but you have a sense where...

Betty Hill: We have to go where they go. Okay, would you like to see a picture of a landed UFO?

Interviewer: Sure, I'd love to.

Betty Hill: Okay, I'll go get it.

Interviewer: I'll keep Junior company. Junior is the clay model depiction of the entity Betty saw on Spetmeber 19th, 1961. Betty, as far as UFO's what's the largest one you've seen. Mother-ships we've heard a mile long, do you believe that?

Betty Hill: Most UFO's are small.

Interviewer: Most UFO's are small, say what, the size of an automobile? An airplane?

Betty Hill: About the size of a car, a little bit bigger. Actually when people say they saw this huge one, it's actually a lot of little ones hooked up together flying in a solid mass. Okay this is a landed one:

Betty's image of landed UFO

Interviewer: Wow, you can actually see pods or three legs of the craft. So this is a landed UFO; New Hamshire.

Betty Hill: Yes.

Interviewer: Looks to be at dawn or dusk or is that the light being given off by the craft?

Betty Hill: It's beginning to get dark.

Interviewer: So, you're looking more or less west for that photo.

Betty Hill: Yes.

Interviewer: What year was thattaken in?

Betty Hill: Probably in the seventies.

Interviewer: Okay in the seventies.

Betty Hill: This one would come in every night and land.

Interviewer: In the same spot?

Betty Hill: Yup, the same general area. And then others would come in, fly up to this one and then go off. So I would call this one the headquarters. This is where they come in to get their orders for the night.

Interviewer: What town? Just give me a hint I know you don't want to sell out where the place is...

Betty Hill: Sorry.

Interviewer: Okay well I tried, I did try didn't I. All we can say is Southern New Hamshire.

Betty Hill: Also this one, actually there is about fourteen lights; sometimes they only have two or three lights. Sometimes, they have red lights, grren lights; see you can see legs on it.

Interviewer: You almost had a feeling of where to go for this one. You had your group together, you had an inkling. Is that what I'm getting, you had an idea, here's where, if we hang out here long enough we're gonna see them.

Betty Hill: No.

Interviewer: No, okay.

Betty Hill: No, driving to my mother's house, now coming from her house at night, usually we would be paced, we would have a UFO on each side of the car and then they would go ahead of us and we would follow them; and they led me to this spot.

Interviewer: Do you have a feeling these are the same entities that originally abducted you on September 19th?

Betty Hill: I don't know but I assume they knew them. I assume they had some kind of record.

Interviewer: Alright, what just from the same squadron so to speak?

Betty Hill: Yup.

Interviewer: So those just land; obviously you didn't walk towards it or touch it or try to get close, the idea was they land, here we are, if you want to take your photos, take them now or...

Betty Hill: Actually if a person tried to walk towards them, they would come up and dart towards the person and scare the person; they leave or sometimes they just take off. They usually, they just sit there.

Interviewer: When was the last time you saw a UFO? This being 1999.

Betty Hill: I looked out the window the other night and of them was flying.

Interviewer: Wow.

Betty Hill: It was a very poor sighting. You know, I could tell it was a UFO because the altitude and speed and lighting.

Interviewer: What do this about cloaking possibilities? I've heard stories that Icould be standing beside somebody that sees UFOs and I can't see them if I'm not at a certain angle.

Betty Hill: If you can't see them, I suggest you have your eyes checked.

Interviewer: Okay.

Betty Hill: You need glasses baby.

Interviewer: So in other words, when they make themselves appear, they appear to everyone not just to certain people.

Betty Hill: Right.

Interviewer: So there's nothing to do with this New Age vibrational...

Betty Hill: I don't know anything about that.

Interviewer: Good, that's another good thing I'm going to put on the T-shirt. Let's talk about now, you get catapaulted as the UFO authority; you're invited abroad. Tell me about Europe's reaction or Soviet Union's reaction and how you were treated and who you met etcetera. If you could maybe give me a brief overview say or when you went to Europe.

Betty Hill: I've even been on TV in China.

Interviewer: Okay.

Betty Hill: In this way; a film that was done here was sold to China and they had somebody speaking Chinese for me. Same thing I'm in Montreal, I'm speaking French. Everywhere I go, I'm speaking the native...

Interviewer: They're dubbing in the voice. So safe to say this phenomenon is worldwide or it's just the interest is worldwide or have youheard from all the remote parts of Europe with people recounting similar incidents to yours. How do you describe this phenomenon.

Betty Hill: Well, oh it's worldwide naturally. Like my sone was in the Navy, stationed in Japan, he had a Japanes wife and then he got transferred to this country and this was in the sixties and she brought with her publications about UFO's in Japan and I still have them.

Appendix 2 – Additional Interview with John McCarthy

Interview with Polygraph Examiner John McCarthy (JM), conducted March 1st, 1977. Interviewer is John Schaefer (JS).

JS: I'm having an interview with John McCarthy and the date is March 1st, 1977. And you had a comment to make on that article?

JM: Yes, it's over questioning Lorenzen, and it says, "Let's talk about the McCarthy polygraph test which was made only a week after Travis returned and which he failed. Why were those results hushed up?" Lorenzen: "Three psychiatrists who examined Travis on the same occasion declared the test to be meaningless because of Walton's state of mind and the circumstances under which the test was given."

Well number one, this is fabrication by Lorenzen because there were no psychiatrists present at the occasion that I ran him. The only people outside of the National Enquirer reporters and photographers who were there were Walton's brother, Travis Walters brother Dwayne and a Dr. Harder. He was introduced to me as a Doctor. I just don't know whether he was a medical doctor or what he was. I found out later, he was something of a psychologist or a hypnotist or something of this nature when actually he's a professor of Engineering, I think something at Cal.

Okay now, those are the only people present. I learned some months later, in fact during the time when I was there in the room with Harder and the rest of them, Harder received a telephone call, I believe from Lorenzen; I'm not sure, in which Harder relayed to the others that doctor's so-an-so, husband and wife team were flying in from Colorado and they'd be in that night or the next day.

I found out late that these were the psychologists who examined him, but they weren't present at the time I gave the examination.

Also Lorenzen is not being very straight-forward in this interview with Oberg. Lorenzne himself made the initial contact with me to do the examination, asked if I would do the examination. And I had been referred to him by a friend of him here in town, for whom I used to work; and who knows of my professionalism in the polygraph field.

So he called me ostensibly as the number one man to do the test. After a brief conversation with Lorenzen on the phone, he said, "I'm going to put Dr. Harder on." So then Harder got on the phone and introduced himself as Dr. Harder and asked if I would be willing to do the test and I said, "yes".

And He said he had hypnotized Walton and I asked him, "Now would that have any effect on the possible outcome of the polygraph examination? Is this man going to be under hypnosis?"

And he said, "Oh no, we just hypnotized him to see if his story was straight," and so forth and so on. "But he's not under hypnosis, and he won't be under hypnosis when the examination takes place."

I asked if he was mentally and physically capable after his alleged incident. And he said, "Oh yes, he's perfectly alright"...or words to that effect. So we agreed to the examination, and that was here in the office. They called me on the phone here.

Later at my home they specified the time and place for the examination, which would be at the hotel in Scottsdale, and that I wasn't to tell anybody where I was going. And I said, "that's fine, except that I shall tell my wife." And they sort of laughed and agreed to that. So, there were no psychiatrists present at the same time, so therefore Lorenzen wasn't being very factual with Oberg on that point.

JS: What APRO affiliated persons were at the Sheraton Hotel during your test?

JM: The only one that I'm aware of was Der. Harder. Lorenzen was not there. The rest of the people there were, as I said, Dwayne Walton and the various photographers and reporters for the National Enquirer.

JS: What was the state of Travis' mind prior to the test?

JM: He appeared to me to be perfectly lucid. We went through a rather extensive pre-test interview, and during this time I sized him up like we do on any examination with anybody, to see if he was; in our opinion, rational and so forth. And he assured me that he was. And he talked and answered my questions rather straight-forwardly.

JS: And so, in your opinion, you would not say that he was unsettled.

JM: No. He was, I would say, apprehensive, as is anybody that is going to go through a polygraph examination. Whether it's for pre-employment or a criminal test for some judge here in town. Everybody's a little apprehensive.

JS: Did you frame your own test questions?

JM: Oh yes.

JS: They did not indicate in advance what areas you should ask, or did they give you any specific questions?

JM: No. They told me what had transpired, and then Dr. Harder indicated they had several tape recordings of interviews with Walton which they had taken.

And I said, "Well, in preparation for this, I'm going to sit down and go over these interviews and listen to these recordings." And they produced several…they ahd about three or four or five tape recorders all over the place.

And so they went to lunch …all of them…and left me in the room. And I sat down there which they were at lunch and listened to the tape recordings and the questions and the answers that Walton gave and I jotted down notes which I thought were pertinent.

Following this, they came back to the suite of rooms, to the bedroom, and they asked if I wanted anything else. And I said, "Yes, I would like to talk to…" they brought

Dwayne in and introduced me to him...and I said, "I'd like to talk to Dwayne before I see Travis."

At this point I had never seen Travis. They had him in another room someplace in the complex. So I cut a short interview with Dwayne, and I asked him about Travis, and what type of kid he was, and had he ever used drugs or anything of this nature,...and he assured me he was a straight arrow,...that he was like a father to him, and he had sort of brought him up over the years; and he had never used drugs and never been in trouble with the law or anything or this nature. He was just a straight kid, and he would never lie to anybody. And so with that, I was introduced to Travis and we started.

JS: Okay. Do you personally feel that there was anything wrong with the type of questions you asked Travis? For example, APRO says Travis was boxed in as your first question forced him to speculate. For example, your question: "Were you actually taken aboard a spacecraft on November 5th, 1975?"

JM: Well, I didn't box him in. I'm just asking him a question to which he previously...a deed which he asserted had happened to him...that was on a spacecraft. So, my first question was, "Were you actually on a spacecraft?"

JS: How do you think APRO can make value judgments against your testing, especially after this rape of polygraph testing standards with George Pfeiffer?

JM: Personally, I don't see that anybody I have talked to in APRO has any experience in the polygraph technique or in the proper framing of testing or anything else. They may talk a lot, but as far as I'm concerned, they don't have any valid premise for their contentions.

JS: Have any of your technical peers criticized your ethics in this case?

JM: No.

JS: Nobody's said anything to the media or anything against your ethical standards?

JM: Not to my knowledge. Oh, that brings up another question. If I recall correctly, Lorenzen told somebody or printed in that APRO bulletin that I had violated our code of ethics because I revealed the fact that he was tested when I was sworn to secrecy, or some such thing like that.

To back up a bit, prior to the examination of Walton, this Jenkins, I believe it was, who was the lead reporter on this team from the National Enquirer, out of their Los Angeles office; asked me if I would have any objection to his photographer taking pictures of myself, the instruments, and the charts, subsequent to my test, and I said, "No, I have no objection whatsoever."

Following the test, and after I had given my adverse opinion, and they got all shook up, there was no mention of any photographs or anything else; but what they did do, they went into a little huddle and went into an adjoining room and typed out a statement which they asked me to sign , saying that I wouldn't reveal their presence, or their investigating team here in town, and that I would not reveal the results of the tests to anyone, except the editor in Florida to whom I was directed to send the report.

And so I did, I signed it. And Jenkins signed it, and some other National Enquirer reporter signed it. Now Lorenzen is claiming that I violated that pact which I signed with the National Enquirer people, because I was the one who revealed the fact that Walton had taken the test and flunked it. Well this is not true.

I have subsequently…the first indication that I knew that anybody else knew that I had done Walton, was that I got a telephone call from Washington, D.C., from Philip Klass, and Phil said that he had been talking to Tom Ezell, whose office is right down the street here and for whom Pfeiffer worked at that time, and concerning Pfeiffer's test of Walton. And Tom Ezell apparently told Phil that he might call me...that he understood that I might have run Walton previously.

And this sort of surprised Phil apparently, and he called me, and asked me point blank...he said he talked to Tom Ezell, and he said, "Did you run a polygraph examination on Travis Walton?" And I'm not going to lie, and I said, "Yes, I did." He said, "Could you tell me when?" And I said, "Last November, what was it, the 15th or some such thing like that." That was in, I believe, March or last year that I got this call.

Subsequently, after Lorenzen came out and accused me of revealing the test and breaching the faith, as it were, I checked with Tom Ezell to find out how he heard that I may have run this guy, and he said that he heard it from Pfeiffer, and the only way that Pfeiffer could have known it was that it came from one of the APRO people...Lorenzen or somebody else, or the Waltons themselves.

So they're the ones who revealed the fact that the test was made and that he flunked it, not me. I really corroborated it when Phil asked me that question, and I don't think that's any breach of faith.

JS: Would it be possible to have your results in testing methodology reviewed by an outside board of polygraph operators, as not to question you, but to put APRO in an uncompromising position?

JM: Certainly, I wouldn't hesitate for a second to turn my charts and the questions over to any qualified polygraph expert.

JS: Do you maintain copies of the questions you ask? Do they go into your personal records that, you know, for a review at a later date exactly word-for-word what is was that you asked?

JM: Yes.

JS: You do have that available now?

JM: Oh yes, I still have the original notes.

JS: Now APRO has made slanderous statements against your character, and what is your response to that?

JM: I don't recall specifically which "slanderous" statements. Can you refresh my memory? Are they outlined here?

Well to begin with , during the pre-test interview, which is done in all instances in every examination, while we're making up the questions...the questions have got to be phrased so they must be answered yes or no...and after the list of questions was made up, I went over these questions with Travis verbatim, asked him if he understood them, and he said, "yes".

Now we went through each one of them, and he was asked to answer yes or no to each one of them before we ever put the instrumentation on him. He was sitting in a chair over there, and I was sitting over here. To each of these questions I asked him, "Can you answer this with a flat yes or no?" "Was that your experience?" And he said, "Yes."

Now, they have documentation on this, because they had at least two tape recorders going in that interview during the entire test. The National Enquirer had one, I think Dr. Harder's was going, and Dwayne had another one mounted right next to where Travis was sitting.

So there were at least two, possibly three tape recordings of all of our conversation. And my interview with him, the stressing of his understanding of each question; could he understand them, yes or no, and so-forth and so-on.

So before we ever started, he agreed that they were all clear, he understood them, and he understood the points that were at issue. He didn't indicate to me that any of them were ambiguous or that he wasn't in the aircraft, or was only awake for two hours, as Lorenzen has indicated. He claimed that he was taken aboard the aircraft and he was there; all the time.

JS: If APRO continues to make any type of slanderous remarks or defamation of your character publicly like this, will there be any action taken on your part?

JM: We have already discussed it with an attorney.

JS: How confidential was the pre-test interview? Was all of that privileged information, and if so, why do you think they wanted to keep it that way?

JM: I don't see how it could be considered privileged information. They were all recording it. I imagine that several copies of those recordings have been made. I wasn't given any indication this was strictly a privileged thing. The only time that...when I was asked to sign this statement; that was after the fact, after they found out that in my opinion he was lying. Then they whipped up this statement for me to sign.

JS: So you feel that the reason for that statement for you to sign was so that it would not get out publicly that he did not pass the polygraph test.

JM: That's right. See, the Enquirer had already come out and said that the boys up in Holbrook had passed an examination by a DPS examiner and that actually they saw him go up in a spacecraft...abducted in a spacecraft and hit by a blue light.

Now I've talked to Mr. Gilson who ran that examination. Mr. Gilson was doing this for, on behest of the sheriff up there, and he wasn't interested in whether or not this guy had been abducted.

They thought that he might have been done away with and a crime had been committed, and this was the gist of the examination on all those boys. Now, at the behest of the sheriff, Mr. Gilson threw in one question about did they actually see a spacecraft or did they think they saw a spacecraft...I forget now the exact terminology.

Now, unfortunately, I think Mr. Gilson will agree with this and his boss over there; this is not good polygraph technique. You can't mix up issues. You've got to stick with one issue. He did not examine these people on the abduction; the spacecraft. He was examining them about the possibility a crime, foul play in the woods and so-forth and so-on. That's why they wanted to search for his body and so-forth.

So it's unfortunate that he threw in one question, did they see a UFO?...or whatever his terminology was. The National Enquirer, when they first came out with this in big headlines, indicated that he had passed the DPS, that all of the boys had passed the DPS examination and they saw him abducted. Big deal...it wasn't so.

Now when I came up with the adverse report, National Enquirer wanted that squashed apparently. This is why Jenkins, I think his name is, had me sign this thing. Because they didn't want us to get out and spoil their little ploy.

JS: APRO has also made a claim that your memory was somewhat faulty regarding the statements Travis made about the entire family, in other words, Dwayne, the mother, and himself regarding seeing UFOs previously.

JM: Well, my memory wasn't faulty. He...in my pre-test interview with him, I asked him if he had been a UFO buff or a believer, whatever term I used, and he said, "Oh, yes". He and his whole family, his brother, and his mother were also interested in them. And subsequent to all this flap, I believe it was Bill Spaulding told me that he had interviewed people up there and that it was known to the populous all over that area that these people were "UFO nuts" and had been for years.

Now I notice in one of Lorenzen's reports that's all been pooh-poohed and they were just kidding people...they didn't really believe in it and so-forth and so-on. I might, if I may, throw in a little other issue here, reference Lorenzen, as long as he is being so critical.

A month or two after my examination of Walton, my wife and I are sitting in our living room watching TV and inadvertently tuned in to this Arizona "Face the State" program, and we immediately became glued, because there was Lorenzen and Walton being interviewed by, I think it was Jim Ryerson of KOOL, in front of a field-stone fireplace effect, so I assumed it was up there in the mountain country, someplace around their home, or in their home. And shortly after we tuned the program in, Ryerson asked Lorenzen how come Walton had never taken a polygraph to clear this thing up.

And he said he'd been examined by doctors, essentially what he's been saying here. Psychiatrists said no, he shouldn't take an examination because he was in such an upset state of mind, therefore no examination was ever given – a bold out-and-out lie.

Now I couldn't remember the exact date of that thing. I called the station and they didn't remember if they had a tape on it or not, but Bill Spaulding did get a tape of it for me and I have it at home. Most interesting - bold faced lie by Lorenzen.

JS: Well apparently it seems that Lorenzen is saying things to cover up his methods of the investigation, where things were not honest and above-board. He's saying things to try and put the blame or make you look bad rather than them.

JM: This appears to be the case. Of course I have no idea what his motives are. But another little...what should you call it...aberration, if you will, came out. Following an interview at the KOOL studios down here, I was introduced to Lorenzen, because it was the first time I had met him. And Travis was there, and Lorenzen introduced me to another fellow who he called his "PR man" from APRO and two or three other people in the area. And we were to be interviewed concerning the test and why my test would be any better than Pfeiffer's test and so-forth and so-on. Well it never got off the ground, really, because every time I started asking a question why Lorenzen or Travis would interject something and start yakking away and we never did...it was a very poorly done interview. I never did get a point across at all.

But, that's not what I'm trying to bring out. After this little taped interview, Ryerson and Lorenzen came up to me while we were standing around there chatting and asked if I could recommend a qualified polygraph expert to do another examination on Walton, and I said, "Yes". And then they, I think they brought up the fact, how about Cleve Baxter? Would he be acceptable? And I said, "Yes, he's very well known, has a wonderful reputation, been in it for years and years and years, and I would recommend him, or John Reed in Chicago, or Lincoln Zohn on the East Coast, or any number of qualified people."

I mentioned a fellow in San Francisco and another one in L.A., and they said, "Well," Ryerson said to me, "Well, I tried to contact Baxter a while back but he was in Brazil." And I said, "Well, he's out of Brazil. He's back in the States because I saw him in August at our American Polygraph seminar in New Orleans."

So this interview was probably...it's got to be after August. It must have been in September or October...sometime last year. And so then Lorenzen and Ryerson seemed to agree on Baxter, and Lorenzen said to me, "How can I get in touch with Baxter?" And I said, "Well, I don't know what his...he's got an office in New York and one in San Diego." I said, "I will send you a letter."I have his telephone number, and address, and everything else here in the office, and I said, "I will look that up for you and send it to you in Tuscon," which I did.

Subsequently, weeks later after they had all been writing…Phil and these people had been writing letters back and forth to agree on the questions and the area and the funding and so-forth for the examination. Phil tells me that Lorenzen sort of fouled up and tripped himself up and he'd already…he said…he told me he didn't know how to get in touch with Baxter, didn't know his address or anything like that, and as it develops, Lorenzen had already been in telephone contact with Baxter prior to our meeting in the studio, period.

So it's another one of his devious things. I don't know why he does this, I don't know.

JS: Well, it seems obvious that he tries to do it to put himself in the best light with the public and to lend credibility to what he is telling the public, and he puts down other people in doing so. And I was just curious as to whether you intend to take any kind of action. You indicated that you have discussed it with an attorney.

Will it go an further than that if he continues to take the course of action he has been taking?

JM: Well, it's in our attorney's hands and what he will recommend, we will follow. Here's another quotation on this Oberg interview that's interesting. So Oberg says, "So McCarthy violated professional ethics in disclosing this information?" Lorenzen: "Yes, he certainly did. A number of his peers feel that his action has damaged the image of his profession. Of major concern to other polygraph operators in the Phoenix area is McCarthy's apparent willingness to go to a news media to disclose confidential information in direct violation of verbal commitment and written contract."

Well, McCarthy didn't go to the news media. After this came out, the news media came to McCarthy. Oh yes, and Holberg says Klass said it wasn't quite that way; he learned of the previous test from Ezell, who had been informed of it through Pfeifer. Klass then called McCarthy up and asked him point-blank if it was true and McCarthy admitted it. Lorenzen: He should have told Klass it was privileged information he should not talk about.

JS: Now, according to this article here, this is from the APRO bulletin, in July of 1976, it says here: "The operator McCarthy was recommended by an APRO member who lives in Phoenix who knew only that McCarthy had long experience in the field.

Mr. Lorenzen made the initial call to McCarthy to determine his willingness to participate. On his affirmative response, Lorenzen turned the phone over to Dr. Harder who discussed that link, the agitated state of mind that Travis was in, and expressed his doubts concerning Travis' testability. McCarthy promised to take this into consideration, and promised complete confidentiality. 'The information will never leak out of this office,' he said, 'you can rest assured of that'. So he's indicating that on this telephone conversation, that you agreed to confidentiality, rather than like you said with the...

JM: That may very well be. They obviously must have taped this thing because they're using that quote verbatim in two or three places.

JS: Okay, and later on down here...

JM: That brings up another question. Is there any violation of law in taping a telephone conversation without the consent of the parties on the other side?

JS: I believe there is. Keep that in mind when you talk to your attorney. It says here: "Another important point now at the constraint of confidentiality is removed, is that test conducted by McCarthy on November 15th, 1975 was unbelievably incompetent." And that's what they've printed on their bulletin right here. Do you have a copy of this yourself?

JM: Yes, Phil sent me a copy of it.

JS: Okay. And that gets into the line of questioning that we discussed earlier. Do you have anything else that you would like to add on your behalf on this incident and whatever has developed as a result?

JM: No, I don't think so. Have you or Bill Spaulding heard any more about any subsequent testing, or is it all off now?

JS: Bill might know something, I personally don't. I'm involved with the quarterly bulletin, Ground Saucer Watch Bulletin, that is put out. That's myself and three other co-editors who put the story together. We'd like to use this interview within our bulletin – nothing to be taken out of context, and a copy of it, should we use it, be given to you so that you have it in your possession exactly what went into it, so that nobody could ever come back and say something else was said other than what was in there. Do you have any objection to our using this?

JM: I have no objection at all.

JS: Well, I don't have any further questions, unless you have anything else you'd like to interject.

JM: No, I don't think so...Oberg questioning Lorenzen again: "What was wrong with the McCarthy tests?" And Lorenzen: "It was unbelievably incompetent. McCarthy broke some of the most elementary rules of polygraph profession. Describing the tests as meaningless as we have done, is really too kind. It was badly botched by McCarthy. Sometimes long years of experience can serve to crystallize bad habits."

Well, I don't know whether he's researched my experience or not, but I have been in the polygraph business here in Arizona longer than any other examiner in the state. I have been qualified as an expert witness in Maricopa County Superior Courts since 1960. I did the narcotics tests in the State vs. Valdez, which resulted in our Supreme Court ruling unanimously in May of 1961, I believe it was, which ruled expert polygraph testimony admissible in any criminal trial in the State of Arizona.

I have been retained by the Attorney General's Office of the State Department of Narcotics and Liquor Control, Highway Patrol, State Prison, County Attorney's Office of Maricopa, Pinal and Yuma Counties, A.S.U., by the Public Defender from Maricopa County and the Federal Public Defender. Also testified as an expert in United States District Court here in Arizona. And if my so called "bad habits" have been crystallized over the years, apparently the courts don't think so. They still recognize me as a qualified expert witness.

JS: Very good. Thank you.

***

Appendix 3 – 1984 MUFON Report on Pascagoula Incident

On October 12,1973, the day after Charles Hickson and Calvin Parker reported being taken aboard a UFO while fishing in Pascagoula, Mississippi, they were taken to Keesler Air Force Base in nearby Biloxi to be interviewed by Air Force officials. The transcript of that interview has never been released, although Air Force officials had promised to send a copy to the sheriff of Jackson County while refusing to give Hickson or his attorney, Joe Colingo, a copy.

Now a copy of that transcript has surfaced, being given to MUFON by Ran Stanford, of Austin, Texas. Stanford said he received a copy of the transcript from the father of one of the Air Force officers who took part in the interview.

Following are major portions of the transcript, which was edited down because of its length.

12 October 1973

The following is a transcription of a report made this date by the following individuals:

Mr. Charles Hickson , Mr. Calvin Parker, Jr.,

The report was made to the following personnel:

Lt. Colonel Derrington, Security Police.
Colonel Amdall, Chairman, Department of Medicine.
Colonel Rudolph, Hospital Service.
Colonel Hanson, Veterinary Services
Lt. Colonel Gibson, Associate Administrator.
Major Winans, Health Physicist.
Captain Hoban, Security Police.
MSgt. Russell, Security Police.
T.E. Huntley, Detective, Jackson County Sheriff's Office,
J o e Colingo , Attorney ,Pascagoula,
Mr. Hickson and Mr. Parker both stated they were employed in Pascagoula by F.B. Walker & Sons,

Two persons who reported sighting an object at approximately the same time were: Raymond Broadus, Probation and Parole Officer, Pascagoula. Larry, Larry's Standard Station, Market & Highway 90, Pascagoula.

Lt. Colonel Derrington: I think the best way is to let them tell it as they recall it and then, on specifics, let them fill in areas for clarification.

Charles Hickson: Yesterday evening— I work at the shipyard and when I come in we decided we would go fishing. And the tide wasn't right and we didn't go out in a boat or anything, we thought we would go down — I don't know whether you are familiar with that area or not where the grain elevator is— on the west bank of the river where the shipyard is. So we fished a while there and didn't have any luck and I told Calvin, who was with me, that we'd goon up the river a little further toward the shipyard. I had fished that area in there and loved fishing in there. We hadn't been there very long — we sat on the bank with our spinning reels — when all of a sudden there was a noise. Well what I just heard was a buzzing. I don't know why I turned around. I guess it was to see what it was. It was a blue light— a real light, bright blue light. It could have been purple or something like that. I mean, I would say it was blue at the time I seen the light. At the time I seen the light it just seemed to stop. I would say it was approximately 25 to 30feet away from us, and I didn't know what to think. I was real frightened. I was scared and I know he (Calvin Parker) was from the appearance he had. It seemed that it didn't have exactly a door. It seemed that one end of it just opened up. Three things came out of it — and they didn't touch the ground — just floating, you know, slowly, a couple of feet off the ground. And I couldn't believe it. I was just —

Derrington: You say three things came out of it. What did these three things appear?

Hickson: At the distance I couldn't tell. I mean, it was just immediately where we were.

Derrington: How large was the item hovering?

Hickson: It wasn't round. It seemed oval shaped and it was approximately 8ft. wide, it was a little longer than that, and it had to be over 8 ft. high. When they approached us — one on each side of my arms — but I didn't feel any sensation at all when it touched me. And amazingly I was just lifted right off the ground.

Derrington: You were lifted right off the ground?

Hickson: I was so scared I didn't pay too much attention to what they were doing to him — that was with him. And they carried me through the — I don't know what it was — and as we were in this thing — anything in there that I know of — if I did I didn't have any sensation of touching anything. The whole room like thing seemed to glow. I didn't see anything like light fixtures —just a glowing inside. There were no chairs or anything that I seen. And I didn't see any instruments, although I seen things that I just can't explain what it was. There was things in there.

Derrington: What time of day was this?

Hickson: It was at night.

Derrington: What time?

Hickson: Well, I don't exactly know what time it was because I don't have a watch. It was quite a while after dark.

Derrington: Quite a while after dark?

Hickson: Yes. I don't know — it resembled an eye — but it was a big thing like a globe — but it just moved all around me.

Derrington: This thing, or individual that came after you, you don't have any feel for what it was?

Hickson: Yes, sir. It had features of a human being, but it didn't have any hands. It had pinchers, or something like that.

Derrington: Could you tell if it looked more mechanical than human?

Hickson: No. I just don't know if it looked mechanical more than human. They were real pale looking to me. And I do remember specifically that on what I thought was their feet, there were no toes or anything like that. It was just almost round. It just seemed like it might have been just skin tight what they had on. But I didn't see any clothes. I don't know if I was so frightened, but I didn't see any kind of hair or anything on them. One of them made just some sort of sound. It is hard to say what kind of sound he did make, but the other two — I never heard one sound. Inside the vehicle I did not hear any sound.

Derrington: You mentioned earlier the sound when this thing approached.

Hickson: A buzzing sound. Calvin Parker: Turned around and it was there.

Detective Huntley: You, said there were eyes, a mouth, and a nose.

Hickson: Yes, I don't know whether you would call it a nose. ,It was something sitting on a body and a sharp thing come out about middle ways of the eyes and it looked like an opening to me underneath, and things on the side like ears, I don't know.

Parker: When they got me and took me toward the ship I passed out but it just looked like a ghost out there. It was like if something came through that wall there. .

Hickson: I don't think I could have possibly lost consciousness while I was inside of it. I don't think I did. I think I was conscious all the time.

Derrington: How long were you onboard?

Hickson: I don't know how long we were on board. There was no sensation of moving or anything. I don't know if we moved. I don't know. After it was all over we couldn't believe it and knew we couldn't convince people of what we seen and we waited a while before we went to the Sheriff's Department and told them. I wanted to get the military in on it. I didn't want any publicity and I didn't want any news people, but after I thought about it awhile I figured that was what I should do.

Derrington: What time would you say elapsed from the beginning until you were released?

Hickson: Oh, it had to be - it's hard to say.

Derrington: Was it hours or minutes?

Hickson: It had to be an hour or so. It had to be that long, but it seemed like an eternity. As far as I know I was conscious but I had no sensations inside of there — I didn't have any power to move.

Derrington: How were you released?

Hickson: They carried me right back out and I was immediately put on the, .ground. I felt no pain and I felt normal. Then the vehicle was gone.

Derrington: During this time do you recall seeing Mr. Parker?

Hickson: I don't recall seeing him until after I was out.

Derrington: You didn't see him onboard?

Hickson: No, sir, I didn't. I don't recall seeing him on board at all. As I said, I was scared partly out. of my mind.

Derrington: When was the first time you noticed Calvin?

Hickson: When they brought me back out on the ground, I believe, is when I seen him again. He was hysterical and sort of looked like he was paralyzed but he suddenly came to his senses.

Derrington to Parker: Before you passed put, do you recall being lifted into the vehicle?

Parker: I recall them getting me and just like a big magnet drawing me to it. I wasn't on the ground — I was off the ground. I don't remember a thing. I just blacked out. I just stood there like I was froze. Then I finally got to where I could move a little bit. It was like a bad dream. I wish it had been a bad dream and it would all be over with. I didn't sleep more than three seconds all night.

Derrington: Do you bringing you back out? recall them

Parker: No, sir. When I came to the ship went 'zzzp' and disappeared.

Derrington: Did you discuss what had happened between you?

Parker: I passed out. I did not remember anything.

Hickson: We discussed what had happened to me. We talked a while trying to decide what to do. We drove to a quick service store and discussed it for almost an hour before we decided to go to the Sheriff's office...

Derrington: Did you have anything to drink any place that someone could have slipped something into your drink?

Hickson: No, sir, because we didn't stop anywhere. I had frozen shrimp that was in the freezer that we were fishing with. We didn't stop anywhere but went straight to the river.

Derrington: What is the relationship between the two of you?

Hickson: He is just a friend. His father and myself back home were real good friends, almost like brothers, and he's been down a couple of weeks now working at the same place that I work...

Derrington: Did you hear any other sounds beside this buzzing sound that you mentioned earlier?

Hickson: The only sound that I heard was one of the things made some type of noise. It wasn't anything that I could distinguish or understand.

Parker: It was just a "mmm."

Derrington: Any dust or....

Hickson: No, sir. I didn't see any dust or anything.

Parker: I don't know how to explain it. It was just as still like, and everything, and then I heard a 'zzzp' just like that, and looked around and blue lights coming, and I paralyzed right there. You know, just like if you walk outside and step on a rattlesnake. Think how you feel. That is just how I felt. I would rather it had been a rattlesnake.

Derrington: No depressions in the area at all after this?

Hickson: No, sir.

Parker: Something else. The craft — it never did set down on the ground itself. It stayed approximately two feet from it.

Hickson: It was off the ground.

Parker: Well, really, they didn't nothing touch it — the ground....

Derrington: No exhaust or anything?

Hickson: I didn't see it. If it was I didn't see it. But as I said, I was quite scared.

Derrington: No attempt to your knowledge to communicate with you in any way?

Hickson: Only unless it was — I don't think it was trying to communicate with us. I think — I don't know — it might have been communicating with the others but I didn't hear any —

Parker: They didn't act like they meant any harm to us.

Hickson: They didn't harm me I know, that I know of.

Parker: They did me physically right now but, you know, not physically but mentally it is about to tear me up.

Derrington: What about curiosity. Did there appear to be any unusual curiosity about the objects?

Hickson: It seemed to me that they knew what they were doing, but they was — I don't know what they were trying to find out but they were trying to find out something about us because —you know — what they done to me, and I don't know what they were doing. Other than that, it seemed that they knew what they were doing.....

Derrington: Is this the first experience of this nature that you have had?

Hickson: Yes, sir. This is the first I have ever had of that nature.

Derrington: Prior to this, have you read or heard about unidentified flying objects?

Hickson: Oh yes. I've read and I've heard. Yes, sir. .

Parker: Not too long ago — now it hadn't been — how long? In the apartments? .

Hickson: Yeah. Not too long ago in Gautier there was one of these.

Parker: And there was at least 13 or 14 witnesses.

Hickson: A dozen families was watching it.

Derrington: But this is the first time you have seen anything like this?

Hickson: Like that, yes, sir.

Derrington: You have never seen anything in the past at a distance that you thought —

Hickson: A while back, there was a dozen families out there that said it could have been a flying object. You know — I don't know if it was a flying object or not.

Derrington: You saw something though?

Parker: Yes, sir. There was about 13 more that did.

Hickson: But it was — what they —what we were looking at that night was a glow. It was a real red glowing thing. It could have been a pier light, I guess — or something like that. But I've never, had any experiences with other things close to something like that.

Derrington: Now,' back to , the description of the object. You said about 8 feet in diameter and ;about —

Hickson: It's a rough guess. I mean, I'd say that there wasn't enough of an area in there that they would have — too many things couldn't have been in there.

Derrington: No protrusion or anything similar to a wing of an aircraft?

Hickson: No, sir. I didn't see anything.

Parker: I could sketch a picture out of the craft itself — you know, just on the outside. The inside I can't, now.

Hickson:. It wasn't round, it was more or less oblong, or something like that. It wasn't completely round.

Derrington: Did you ever hear any motor sounds?

Hickson: Nothing but just the little buzzing is all that I heard.

Derrington: Did it buzz all of the time or just when it moved?

Hickson: No, sir. When it moved. Inside of it I didn't hear any sound from the vehicle or whatever it was. I didn't hear any sound from it while I was in there.

Derrington: About how tall were these things?

Hickson: Well, it's hard to tell about everything. It had to — it was tall enough that when we went in the opening we weren't touching anything.

Derrington: I mean the individuals.

Hickson: I'd say somewhere approximately 5 feet, or something like that.

Parker: Of course you know they wasn't on the 'ground so that made them taller than us. You know — as far as getting out walking across, the ground.

Hickson: When you are that frightened it's hard to give a good description of something. .

Derrington: You talked about them moving. Did they move with leg motion or —

Parker: Drifted.

Hickson: Just flying. .

Parker: Like if wasn't no gravity around.

Hickson: I didn't see any motion of their legs but I know they had motion with what I guess was arms — I guess it was arms because they moved them whenever they lifted me.

Parker: And it was like a crawfish or crab.

Derrington: Was anything strapped on this, like a sort of pack or anything?

Hickson: I didn't see anything like that.. Just the thing, is all.

Derrington: Just the body frame of the individual and it was either unclothed or clothed with something very tight fitting?

Hickson: Yes.

Derrington: Did this creature have two arms and two legs, or what seemed to be?

Hickson: It seemed to be two of each one. Yes, sir.

Parker: But it wasn't like our arms and legs. You know, well it was on the same basic manner as an arm and leg but it wasn't physically looking the same.

Huntley: I believe you told me that it looked more like a crab claw.

Parker: Yes sir.

Hickson: The guy had claw like things. It wasn't fingers like our fingers are....

Derrington: Were there any windows in the craft?

Hickson: I couldn't see anything from inside of it. I don't know...

Derrington: Did it go straight up?

Parker: No sir. It just disappeared... 'zzzp' and it just disappeared.

Hickson: And really, I don't know how it got there.

Major Winans: Did it seem to be plastic, or transparent, or was it solid looking material?

Hickson: It had a glow and I couldn't tell whether it was solid or transparent. I couldn't give you no details of that at all because I don't know.

Winans: Was it glowing from the inside or from the outside?

Hickson: It was glowing — it was bluish like on the outside and on the inside it was just like — you know, like light.

Winans: Just like in this room here with the fluorescent color? Same color?

Hickson: Yes, only there was no bulbs, globes, or anything.

Winans: Did you feel the same temperature, or did you feel warm?

Hickson: I didn't have any sensation —any feeling at all.

Amdall: Did you feel like you could have moved?

Hickson: I couldn't move.

Derrington: What went on while you were inside?

Hickson: Well, then — as I said before, they had something — I still say an eye— which I know it wasn't an eye — but, it just circulated around — around by me — and they could do me any way they wanted to — lay me back, or sideways.

Derrington: This eye that was under you — you were under constant observation by this eye while you were on the board?

Hickson: Yes. I say an eye. I don't mean it in that respect. Well, when something is looking at me like that I guess you would figure you would have to say it's some kind of an eye. It didn't look like a camera or anything like that.

Huntley: Now when you were stretched out — I believe you said you were stretched out. Right?

Hickson: At one time, yes, sir.

Huntley: Did you say — didn't you tell us that they moved the light over you —back and forth and all over your body?

Hickson: The thing moved all back over me and all around me.

Derrington: Did it move by itself?

Hickson: It moved by itself to the best I can remember. I was so darned scared till I don't really know whether I lost consciousness. I don't think I did. I don't think I lost consciousness. I think I was conscious all the time — I believe I was — that I was in there.

Winans: Did the projector have any sort of an arm to it?

Hickson: I don't know. It didn't seem to be attached to anything. It could have been. I don't know.

Derrington: When you regained consciousness, where did you go first? After you left this area?

Hickson: Well, we went over across —we live in Gautier. We stopped over there at the — close to the Li'l General Curb Market and talked about it a longtime again.

Derrington: What time was this now?

Hickson: Oh, this must have been —aw heck, it was around 10 or 11 o'clock, or something like that.

Huntley: They came into the Sheriff's office at, I believe, 11:18...

Amdall: Have either of you been on any medication or any kind of drugs?

Hickson: No, sir.

Parker: No, sir. I haven't.

Derrington: What about alcohol?

Parker: I don't drink.

Hickson: Well, I take a drink occasionally and after that happened last night — after I left the Sheriff's Department, I got home and I even took a drink to try to relax and it didn't even relax me. I drink occasionally', yes.

Derrington: But you had had nothing to drink prior to this?

Hickson: No, sir.

Winans: How did you get that mark on the tip of your little finger?

Hickson: This is a blister, you know —from some hot steel. No, it is not related to this at all.

Huntley: Calvin had a couple of little small scratches on this right arm. When he mentioned something about a claw and I noticed that he said he grabbed him by both arms and I noticed that both arms have a little scratch.

Hickson: Well, I couldn't find any scratches at all on me. There's no marks at all that I — I didn't find any on me at all.

Parker: There wasn't no feeling to the thing. You just couldn't feel nothing. It's a wonder I didn't hurt myself when I came through this.

Attorney Colingo: I can say this. Not this particular story, but at the same time, this object was sighted by others who are as critical or — well by officers. One man was Broadus. He related the story again this morning at the police station where they were going down the highway and passed the vicinity where. they were. You can see it from the, highway there just across the bridge. They saw the object for three minutes. And the times correspond. . .;

Huntley: And their description and everything. They even described the blue lights and everything.

Hanson: Was it a dark blue light or a light blue light?

Hickson: It was just a glowing... don'tknow.

Colonel Rudolph: Had they had the opportunity to hear the tape before reporting this?

Huntley: Yes.

Colingo: Oh, they have heard it now. Do you mean did they know?

Huntley: Yes. The tape — I took the tape, or they did, last night: I played it back...

Rudolph: Before they gave their report?

Colingo: Did Broadus come and report this sighting and then these men?

Huntley: I don't remember now. I would have to check with the chief on that. But I do know that they heard the tape that we took last night — or they took last night.

Rudolph: This was after they had been in to tell their story?

Huntley: Right. Then that is when they said, "Well, you know that is funny because we saw the same thing. We saw a blue light." In fact Mr. Broadus is a Christian man and he said he'd been over to Gautier somewhere to church.

Colingo: If Mr. Broadus says he saw it— he saw it. I mean, he is that type of fellow. Now this other fellow — I don't know who you are talking about.

***

Bibliography & References

The Interrupted Journey – Two Lost Hours Aboard a Flying Saucer
By John Fuller

A Dramatic UFO Encounter in the White Mountains, New Hampshire - The Hill Case - Sept. 19-20,1961
By Walter N. Webb

Captured! The Betty and Barney Hill UFO Experience
By Stanton T. Friedman and Kathleen Marden

MUFON Case Files: www.mufon.com

Project Blue Book Archive: www.bluebookarchive.org

Also available on Amazon by Sean Keyhoe:

Are Aliens Real? Aliens and UFOs Proof

http://www.amazon.com/dp/B00BL2MPNG

Printed in Great Britain
by Amazon.co.uk, Ltd.,
Marston Gate.